Vietnam Air War:

25 Rarely Told Stories

To Alex, Carrie,
Gabriel & Jayden,

with compliments
of the compiler,

Erhard

Erhard Konerding holds a B.A. degree in history from Long Island University and Masters degrees from Columbia and Wesleyan Universities. He is Documents Librarian at Wesleyan University in Middletown, Connecticut. Always interested in military history, Mr. Konerding has studied the History and Sociology of Warfare and is an expert on military hardware.

Other Southfarm Press books by Erhard Konerding:
Vietnam War Facts Quiz: 21st Century Edition (2006)
    ISBN-13: 978-0-913337-58-5
World War II Facts Quiz: Europe (2006) ISBN-13: 978-0-913337-59-2
World War II Facts Quiz: The Pacific (2006) ISBN-13: 978-0-913337-60-8

Other Southfarm Press Air War books:
Flying Low: And shot down twice during World War II in a spotter plane by Joseph Furbee Gordon (2001) ISBN-13: 978-0-913337-62-2 (2006 ed.)
The Grasshopper That Roared by Jean L. Chase (2005)
    ISBN-13: 978-0-913337-54-7
Janey: A Little Plane in a Big War by Alfred W. Schultz (1998)
    ISBN-13: 978-0-913337-31-8

Vietnam Air War:

25 Rarely Told Stories

Compiled by
Erhard Konerding

Southfarm Press, Publisher
www.war-books.com
Middletown, Connecticut

ISBN-13: 978-0-913337-63-9
ISBN-10: 0-913337-63-3

Illustrations are courtesy of Associated Press,
Bell Helicopter/Textron, Boeing Helicopter Company, Cessna,
Department of Defense Still Media Records Center,
Lockheed-Georgia Company, Rockwell International,
United States Air Force and United States Navy

Every effort has been made to locate the copyright holders
of all copyrighted materials and to secure the necessary
permission to reproduce them. In the event of any questions
arising as to their use, the publisher will make
necessary changes in future printings.

Attention: Educational Institutions and Veteran's Organizations
Southfarm Press books are available at quantity discounts
with bulk purchase for use as educational materials and premiums.
For information, please write to Special Sales Department
at our address shown above.

Visit our Web Site at <u>www.war-books.com</u>

This book is dedicated to all the American men and women
who served in Vietnam,
whether in the air, on the ground, or on a ship off-shore.

CONTENTS

Introduction

The Vietnam War saw the use of aircraft on an unprecedented scale. The helicopter, particularly, came into its own in a variety of roles. American airmen fought bravely, often at the cost of their lives, whether bombing the North or South, directing artillery fire, flying fighter cover or bombers, rescuing downed air crew or ground troops, airlifting men and cargo in dangerous areas, or quietly resisting as prisoners of war.

Using official unclassified U.S. government sources, Erhard Konerding, documents librarian at Wesleyan University, Middletown, Connecticut, researched, edited and included in the book over 25 rarely told stories involving aircraft and crews.

Some of these stories were written during the Vietnam War. Others appeared in official histories and studies written for the Army, Air Force, Navy and Marine Corps.

Konerding does not attempt to include stories about every type of aircraft that participated in the hostilities in Vietnam. He selected representative types of aircraft and includes a true story for each.

Historians, veterans, aircraft buffs and model builders will find the stories, photographs and aircraft specifications of interest. Since aircraft weights, speeds and armament vary with subtypes and missions, the technical specifications included usually represent the specific aircraft model described.

A complete list of sources appears at the end of the book.

CHOPPERS

Choppers as Gunships

Before the Vietnam War, there were many people, both in and out of the military, who didn't understand the role of the armed helicopter. Ever since Colonel Jay D. Vanderpool had tied a machine gun on a H-13 in the mid-50's, there were those who saw the armed helicopter as a fragile toy dreamed up by frustrated fighter pilots in the Army who were unable by regulation and budget to own really sophisticated attack aircraft. The consensus was generally that a semi-skilled skeet shooter or even a good slingshot artist could knock any helicopter out of the sky at short range and that an encounter with more sophisticated antiaircraft weapons would be suicidal. This attitude is quite understandable in duck hunters who never had the challenge of ducks shooting back. Also, the very nature of the helicopter, ugly and fragile compared to sleek jet aircraft, adds to the conviction that flying one in combat is non-habit forming.

On the plus side, the helicopter is the most agile of all aircraft and has a capability of taking advantage of cover and concealment at extremely low altitudes that would be impossible in a fixed-wing airplane. It was soon proven that the helicopter was remarkably hard to shoot down and the most vulnerable part was the pilot himself. Personnel armor protection and armed seats greatly increased the pilot survivability. The experienced pilot used every unique aspect of the helicopter's flight envelope to his advantage.

Observation from the helicopter is unequaled. The enemy learned that to fire at one was to give up his advantage of cover and concealment and generally bring a devastating return of machine gun fire and rockets. A corollary to the advantage of seeing the enemy was the ability to identify our own troops with precision. Consequently, the armed helicopter pilot could safely place fires within a few meters of our own troops. This became particularly important as the enemy developed the "hugging" tactics which he used to avoid the heavier fires from our tactical air support and B-52 bombers.

The Bell UH-1 Huey (officially "Iroquois") helicopter appears in many photographs, stories, movies and television programs about Vietnam; the versatile Hueys seemed to be everywhere, as troop carriers, transports, Medevac casualty evacuation craft, and even as heavily armed and armored gunships.

UH-1 Huey gunships typically carried several machine guns, 2 rocket pods, and often, automatic grenade launchers. Gunships escorted road convoys and flights of "slicks" (troop carrier helicopters) or provided close support for ground actions.

Manufacturer: Bell
Official name: Iroquois
Crew: 2
Dimensions: Rotor diameter: 44 ft.; Fuselage length: 42 ft.;
Height: 12 ft., 7 in.
Weight: 9,000 lbs. loaded
Speed: 148 mph max.
Armament: 4 7.62-mm machine guns, 2.72 in. rocket pods, 40-mm grenade launcher
Services used by: US Army, USAF, USN, USMC, VNAF

UH-1 Huey Gunship

An incident occurred in southern Quang Ngai Province in late 1967 which demonstrated both the firepower of the armed UH-1E and the tenacity, skill, and courage of Marine gunship crews. On August 19th, Captain Stephen W. Pless, a VMO-6 gunship pilot, was flying chase for an emergency medevac mission when he heard over the radio net of another emergency situation. Pless learned that four U.S. Army soldiers were stranded on a beach north of Duc Pho and were about to be overwhelmed by a large Viet Cong force. Breaking off from his original mission, the Huey pilot flew to the scene. On arrival, Pless saw about 50 VC in the open; some were bayoneting and beating the Americans. He swept in on the VC, killing and wounding many and driving the survivors back into a treeline. He made his rocket and machine gun attacks at such low levels that fragments from his own ordnance pelted the gunship. Though still under heavy small arms fire, Pless landed his gunship between the Communists in the treeline and the wounded soldiers. His two enlisted crewmen, Gunnery Sergeant Leroy N. Poulson and Lance Corporal John G. Phelps, leaped out of the helicopter and raced through enemy fire to help the wounded men.

Captain Rupert E. Fairfield, Jr., the co-pilot, killed three of the nearest VC with a burst from a M-60 machine gun, then ran to help Poulson and Phelps drag the soldiers to the aircraft. Captain Pless hovered his UH-1E and sent streams of machine gun fire into the Viet Cong positions in the treeline. Under cover of his fire, the three crewmen pulled the wounded soldiers into the helicopter. Pless headed the dangerously overloaded aircraft out to sea. Four times the helicopter settled into the water. Each time Captain Pless skipped it back into the air. While the crew threw out all unnecessary gear to lighten the craft, Pless jettisoned the rocket pods. Gradually, the UH-1E gained altitude and limped back to the 1st Hospital Company's landing pad at Chu Lai. In addition to rescuing the Americans, the crew received credit for killing a confirmed total of 20 VC and probably killed another 38. Fairfield, Poulson, and Phelps each received the Navy Cross; Captain Pless received the Medal of Honor.

Medevac missions, named Dust Off by the Army, saved many wounded GI's. Hueys, usually marked by the red crosses often used as aiming points by Vietcong and North Vietnamese gunners, could pick up casualties under fire, and fly them to well-equipped hospitals in a fraction of the time required for ground transport.

Manufacturer: Bell
Crew: 2 to 4
Dimensions: Rotor diameter: 48 ft.; Fuselage length: 44 ft., 7 in.; Height: 13 ft., 5 in.
Weight: 9,500 lbs. loaded
Speed: 160 mph
Armament: 2 7.62-mm machine guns
Services used by: US Army, USAF, USMC, USN, VNAF

UH-1 Huey Medevac

In the late afternoon on January 5, 1968, a company of the 198th Light Infantry Brigade, 23d Infantry Division, operating on the floor of the Hiep Duc Valley, came under a concerted attack by six companies of the 2d North Vietnamese Division. For nine hours from their well-fortified positions in the surrounding hills, the North Vietnamese rained mortars and rockets on the Americans. The enemy had covered the likely flight paths into the area with 12.7-mm. antiaircraft guns. Early in the assault they had shot down two American gunships. Difficult communications and the nearness of the enemy on the night of the fifth had made a Dust Off mission impossible, even though the enemy had inflicted heavy casualties on the Americans. By dawn the company had sixty wounded on its hands.

On the morning of the sixth, a Dust Off pilot Warrant Officer Charles D. Schenck, starting from fire support base West overlooking the valley, tried to fly a medical team out to the company and bring some of the wounded back. But the vertigo he suffered from the zero visibility forced him to abort. Shortly after he returned and told Dust Off Operations Control of his failure, Major Patrick H. Brady and Dust Off 55 began to prepare for flight. Brady, who knew the Hiep Duc Valley, listened to Schenck and the other pilots who had tried to reach the stranded company. Then he loaded a medical team in his ship, cranked the engine, and took off. Several miles from the battle area he found a hole in the soupy clouds through which he descended to treetop level. After twenty long minutes of low-level flight, Dust Off 55 neared the stricken company. Brady's surprise approach and the poor visibility threw off the enemy's aim; the helicopter landed safely.

Once on the ground the medical team quickly found and loaded the most seriously wounded. Brady made an instrument takeoff through the clouds, flew to fire base West, and delivered his casualties to the aid station. He then briefed three other crews on how he would execute his next trip into the area. The three ships tried to follow Brady in, but thick fog and enemy fire made them all climb out and return to West. Brady kept going, landed, picked up a load of wounded, and flew them out to West. Twice more he hovered down the trail and brought out wounded. Although the three other ships again tried to emulate his technique, none could make it all the way. Brady and his crew evacuated eighteen litter and twenty-one ambulatory patients on those four trips. Nine of the soldiers certainly would not have survived the hours which passed before the fog lifted.

As soon as Dust Off 55 refueled, Brady was sent on an urgent mission to evacuate the U.S. soldiers from a unit surrounded by the enemy twenty-six kilometers southeast of Chu Lai. Machine guns swept the landing zone as the North Vietnamese tried to wipe out the remaining American troops. Brady tried another surprise tactic. He low-leveled to the area, dropped in, turned his tail boom toward the heaviest fire to protect his cockpit, and hovered backward toward the pinned soldiers. The ship took rounds going in and once it was on the ground the fire intensified. For fear of being wounded or killed themselves, the friendly forces would not rise up and help load the casualties. Seeing this, Brady took off and circled the area until the ground troops radioed him in a second time. As he repeated his backward hover, the enemy tried once more to destroy the aircraft. But this time the ground troops loaded their comrades, who were soon in the rooms of the 27th Surgical Hospital at Chu Lai.

AH-1 Huey Cobra Gunship

The AH-1 Huey Cobra gunship combined many of the components of the proven UH-1 series with a slim new armored fuselage. More weapons stations, and a rotating grenade launcher turret increased the firepower of the Cobra over its older sibling. AH-1s even took on North Vietnamese tanks, knocking out several with rockets.

Manufacturer: Bell
Crew: 2
Dimensions: Rotor diameter: 44 ft.; Fuselage length: 44 ft., 5 in.;
Height: 13 ft., 7 in.
Weight: 9,400 lbs.
Speed: 172 mph max.
Armament: 1 7.62-mm minigun, 40-mm grenade launcher, 2.75 in. rockets, optional TOW missiles
Services using: US Army, USMC, VNAF

During the 1968 Tet Offensive, there is no doubt that the quick reaction of the armed helicopters saved Tan Son Nhut Airbase and Bien Hoa from serious danger of being overrun. In the first few hours they were the only airborne firepower since the Air Force aircraft could not get clearance to even take off. An Air Force sergeant describing the action on a tape recorder at Tan Son Nhut kept repeating over and over, "Oh, those beautiful Huey gunships!" One of the men in those gunships, Captain Chad C. Payne, a fire team leader, said, "I received fire everywhere I turned. My ships received seven hits, but this was nothing considering the amount of ground fire directed toward us. There were hundreds of VC bodies everywhere in the vicinity of the Tan Son Nhut perimeter. I've never seen anything like it."

Another tribute to the effectiveness of the gunships came from a member of Advisory Team 100 at Tan Son Nhut. When he received word that Tan Son Nhut was under attack, he assembled a patrol of 30 men. "And we ran head-on into one of the attack forces. There were approximately 350 men against my 30. We were certainly outnumbered," he said. "Then those beautiful gunships came in and started circling the area. I threw up a pocket flare to mark the position, and the gunship radioed that we were too close to the enemy force and to pull back some, if possible. We pulled back and then he went in. He was right on target, placing rockets right in the middle of Charlie's position. We killed over 200 enemy, and I'd estimate that 80-85 percent was attributable to the helicopters. The morning of the 31st, if I had met that pilot, I'd have kissed him."

Another area of heavy activity was at the U.S. Embassy in downtown Saigon. Chief Warrant Officer Richard Inskeep of the 191st Assault Helicopter Company was the first to land a chopper on the embassy during the heavy fight, bringing ammunition and evacuating one wounded man. "We were receiving fire from all sides," said Mr. Inskeep, "but we couldn't see anybody around so we lifted off. My gunner than spotted someone in a hole of the roof, so we made a tight turn and came back onto the pad. The fire was so intense that the gunner and crew chief had to pull the ammunition out of the ship and crawl across the roof as they pushed it in front of them. They pushed the ammunition down the hole and helped bring the wounded man back across the roof to the ship."

Watching from below was Mr. George Jacobson, Mission Coordinator of the U.S. Embassy. Commenting on the helicopter's approach, Mr. Jacobson said, "He came in low and I thought for a minute he was going to hit the building, but at the last minute he pulled up and made a beautiful landing on the roof. Afterwards I realized that he did it on purpose to avoid the enemy fire. It was a tremendous piece of airmanship." Mr. Jacobson, a retired Army colonel, was to finish off the last guerrilla inside the embassy. As troopers of the 101st were landed on the Embassy's helipad, the enemy guerrilla tried to escape the troopers, spotted Mr. Jacobson, and fired three shots. He missed and Jacobson shot him with a .45 that had quickly been tossed up to his second floor window by troops below. This was the finale to the six and one-half hour battle within the embassy.

As daylight came over the Bien Hoa Air Base, fighting was still raging around the airfield. Small bands of Vietcong had managed to penetrate the southeast and southwest areas of the air base, and reaction forces were sent out to stop them. The Air Force's 3d Security Squadron found an estimated 100 Vietcong to be in the southwest area just beyond the taxiway. The Vietcong were well dug in, and the security force could not flush them out. On finding themselves pinned down, they called on the Cobras of the 334th Armed Helicopter Company to suppress the guerrillas. Air Force Second Lieutenant John A. Novak, who was in command of the security force, said, "As the Cobras came to our support they swept down about two feet over our heads and fired into the enemy position, knocking out the enemy who were pinning us down. I personally witnessed time after time the Cobras sweep into the VC area and pin down the enemy in the face of heavy fire being directed at them. The Cobras were the turning point in the enemy's destruction."

Search and Rescue

Following the words of their motto "That Others May Live", Air Force rescue crews risked their lives to find and return airmen downed over South and North Vietnam. The helicopters became progressively larger, more powerful, and more heavily armed and armored as the war progressed.

The USAF used the Huskie for firefighting and rescue at stateside bases and sent some to South Vietnam as the first rescue helicopters. They served well, but the Air Force replaced them with bigger, better-armed, and better-equipped craft.

Manufacturer: Kaman
Former Navy and Marine Corps designations: HUK, HOK
Crew: 2
Dimensions: Rotor diameter: 47 ft.; Fuselage length: 25 ft., 2 in.;
Height: 15 ft., 7 in.
Weight: 6,500 lbs. loaded
Speed: 120 mph max.
Armament: 1 7.62-mm machine gun
Service using: USAF

HH-43 Huskie

On June 23, 1965, Major Robert Wilson's F-105 was hit by ground fire while on a mission over southwestern North Vietnam. Wilson could not fly his damaged Thunderchief over a ridgeline, so he ejected. After a normal descent he found himself suspended upside down in a tree 150 feet above the jungle floor. Wilson managed to swing into a crotch of the tree where he wiggled out of his parachute harness. He then took out his survival knife and cut a small branch from the tree. Wilson used the branch to snag his seat pack which contained all his survival equipment. After drawing the pack over to where he stood, he retrieved his survival radio. Wilson contacted the HC-54 airborne rescue command post called "Crown" which, in response to his mayday, had moved off its orbit along the Thai-Laotian border and now flew nearby. Half an hour later four Air Force A-1 Skyraiders droned into view and contacted the survivor. Soon the pilots spotted Wilson's chute and, after radioing the downed pilot's exact position to Crown, flew to an orbit several miles away so as not to reveal Wilson's location to any enemy troops that might be lurking nearby. Had Wilson or the A-1 pilots spotted the enemy, the A-1s would have attacked them with 20-mm cannon fire, rockets, and fragmentation bombs. Ninety minutes after Wilson's ejection, an HH-43, from a forward operating base in Laos, showed up. Wilson fired off a small flare that was part of his survival equipment. The Huskie pilots spotted it and moved their chopper directly overhead while the parajumper lowered the penetrator through the foliage. Wilson grabbed it, strapped himself on, and began his ascent to the helicopter. A few hours later, safe at the Nakhon Phanom officer's club, Wilson set up drinks for the chopper pilots.

Of course not all HH-43 rescue missions went so smoothly, and the enemy sometimes bested the search and rescue task forces. On September 20, 1965, Captain Willis E. Forby's F-105 was hit by large caliber antiaircraft fire while attacking a target near Vinh, North Vietnam. Forby turned his damaged F-105 toward Laos and ejected a few minutes later. His wingman circled until he received a signal from the downed pilot's survival radio indicating he was alive. Then Crown launched two HH-43s. All seemed normal as Captain Forby dispensed smoke to mark his exact location and make voice contact with one of the rescue choppers piloted by Captain Tom J. Curtis. Forby did not know that enemy troops had hidden themselves in the jungle all around to make him the live bait on a flak trap. Captain Curtis was concentrating on holding the chopper in a hover near the survivor when several black clad figures stepped from the underbrush and fired their automatic weapons. The helicopter shivered as bullets impacted, then it dropped into the trees. In an almost automatic response, the pilot of the second helicopter, orbiting above as part of the search and rescue task force, moved in to pick up any survivors as A-1s blasted the surrounding area. Again the troops opened fire forcing the backup chopper to pull up and return to base. Crown called for a massive rescue task force but the armada of A-1s failed to find any trace of the downed men. Tom Curtis spent the next seven years as a prisoner of war in North Vietnam. His copilot, First Lieutenant Duane W. Martin remained a prisoner of the Pathet Lao. Martin escaped captivity a year later, but was murdered by a Laotian peasant before he could be rescued.

HH-3 Jolly Green

The HH-3 "Jolly Green Giant", counterpart to the Navy SH-3 Sea King filled the need for an armed and armored rescue chopper capable of defending itself in a hostile environment. Rescue missions were escorted by fixed-wing aircraft, but the HH-3s still needed to protect themselves during the tense moments of actual low-altitude retrieval of personnel.

Manufacturer: Sikorsky
Crew: 3
Dimensions: Rotor diameter: 62 ft.; Fuselage length: 57 ft., 3 in.;
Height: 18 ft., 1 in.
Weight: 18,000 lbs. loaded
Speed: 162 mph max.
Armament: 2 7.62-mm machine guns

It was the familiar flak trap pattern that developed in the pre-dawn darkness of November 9, 1967. Captain Gerald O. Young, pilot of the Sikorsky HH-3E Jolly Green Giant rescue helicopter, knew his job would be difficult. The previous day a North Vietnamese battalion had ambushed a combined U.S.-Vietnamese reconnaissance team near Khe Sanh, a large Marine combat base in northern Quang Tri Province. Instead of finishing off the survivors the communists used

them for bait for their heavy machine guns which soon brought down a Vietnamese helicopter and a U.S. Army helicopter gunship.

Captain Young was flying backup for another Jolly Green that had been severely damaged while moving in to pick up survivors a few minutes before. Because the ground fire was so intense, rescue coordinators in Saigon authorized Young to abort the mission if he felt it too dangerous.

As Army helicopter gunships led a renewed attack on the enemy, Young worked his Jolly Green into position for the pickup. Enemy bullets slammed into the armor-plated HH-3 as the large helicopter hovered precariously a few feet above the ground while survivors climbed aboard. Then, as its turbines strained and the aircraft reached upward for darkness and safety, an enemy rifle grenade exploded near the starboard engine, causing a blast that flipped the Jolly Green on its back and sent it rolling down a ravine.

Captain Young fell free of the burning, tumbling wreckage and slid to the bottom of the ravine. In spite of burns covering a quarter of his body, Young climbed back up to the mangled chopper halfway down the steep incline. There he found a badly injured airman and carried him into the bushes to hide from the enemy, while he administered first aid. Since enemy troops might be lurking in the area, Young did not dare risk hauling the injured man back up the ravine to join five other survivors huddled near the wreckage. At dawn a pair of single-engine A-1E Skyraiders, called Sandys, appeared overhead and located the men near the burned-out hulk. Fearing another flak trap, the Sandys made forty low-level passes over the area for a period of two hours . . . a tactic called "trolling for fire." After two hours without enemy fire a Jolly Green moved in to pick up the five survivors.

Although the beeper on Captain Young's survival radio functioned normally, he could not establish voice contact with the rescue force, so they were unaware of his exact location at the bottom of the ravine with the injured survivor. After the Jolly Green pulled away, he figured the enemy would return to use him for flak bait as they had the ambushed patrol. Determined not to allow this, Young concealed the injured survivor in the underbrush and struck out through the tall elephant grass hoping to lead the enemy away so that the injured man might be rescued. The trick worked, and the enemy picked up his trail away from the crash site.

Unfortunately, due to the malfunctioning survival radio, the overhead rescue forces were unaware of Young's intentions. Helicopters airlifted a 100-man ground party into the area to pick up bodies and search for survivors. They located the injured man but found no trace of the captain who by this time had led the North Vietnamese several miles away from the crash site. With enemy troops in pursuit, Young stumbled through the bush, sometimes nearly slipping into shock, but refusing to reveal his position to the rescue forces overhead until he was certain a flak trap had not been set up around him. He evaded the enemy throughout the night and finally, on the morning of November 10, he spotted a helicopter circling nearby. The exhausted and injured captain dragged himself into a clearing, was sighted and rescued.

HH-53 Super Jolly Green

This giant helicopter was designed as a troop transport and cargo helicopter. The Air Force chose it as a rescue chopper due to its size and power, which permitted heavier armor and armament and a larger crew.

Manufacturer: Sikorsky
Unofficial name: Big Mother
Crew: 3
Dimensions: Rotor diameter: 72 ft., 3 in.; Fuselage length: 67 ft., 2 in.; Height: 24 ft. 11 in.
Weight: 37,000 lbs. loaded
Speed: 195 mph. max.
Armament: several 7.62-mm machine guns

Among rescue efforts during the Vietnam War, the evacuation of 132 American and Vietnamese troops from the citadel at Quang Tri stands out as one of the largest rescue operations. At the height of the invasion, four North Vietnamese divisions surrounded Quang Tri City cutting off the American advisors and South Vietnamese troops in the old citadel.

On May 1, 1968, four HH-53s from the 37th Aerospace Rescue and Recovery Squadron at Da Nang took off for Quang Tri. They planned to have three Jolly Green Giants pick up all the survivors while the fourth chopper hovered outside the city, ready to dash in if needed. The North Vietnamese had moved SA-2 surface-to-air missiles south and their area of coverage encompassed Quang Tri City. Consequently the helicopters had to approach the city at tree-top level. At that low altitude they ran the risk of automatic weapons fire which they usually avoided by flying above 3,000 feet.

Over the nearly-demolished outskirts of the city, three Jolly Greens moved into a single file to proceed up a corridor blasted by the A-1s to the walls of the fortress. As the first chopper settled into the citadel, enemy small arms fire increased to an intensity that caused so much confusion that only thirty-seven men managed to climb aboard before the pilot pulled away. Staff Sergeant Robert LaPinte, a pararescueman, remained behind to organize the remaining survivors. With order restored, the next chopper loaded forty-five people and quickly took off.

The third Jolly Green into the fortress loaded fifty people just as quickly as the second helicopter. Its pilot pulled up and headed for safety. When it seemed that the rescue effort had ended, Capt. Donald A. Sutton, commander of the backup helicopter, received a frantic radio message, "Hey, we've got more people down here!" Sutton rushed to the citadel, landed, and lowered his ramp. No one ran to the waiting chopper. Suddenly, North Vietnamese troops leaped from the wrecked buildings and opened fire on the sitting Jolly Green. Sutton realized he had been suckered into a trap. As his parajumper blasted everyone in sight with the minigun, the last Jolly rose from the fallen fortress and headed for Da Nang. Minutes later the North Vietnamese flag flew over the citadel's ruins.

CH-46 Sea Knight

Evolved from the "Flying Banana" tandem-rotor helicopter series, the CH-46 was the Marine Corps' standard transport and troop carrier helicopter throughout the Vietnam conflict, suffering many losses due to heavy enemy fire.

Manufacturer: Boeing Vertol
Crew: 3, plus 25 passengers
Dimensions: Rotor diameter: 50 ft.; Fuselage length: 44 ft., 10 in.; Height: 16 ft., 8 in.
Weight: 18,700 lbs. loaded
Speed: 160 mph max.
Armament: None
Services using: USMC, USN

When helicopters proceeded to the hills singly or in small groups, each mission was a hair-raising experience during the Battle for Khe Sanh. A good example of what often transpired during those frantic moments occurred early in the siege on Hill 881S when Captain Dabney called for a chopper to evacuate a badly wounded Marine. One corporal was assigned as a stretcher bearer because he had a badly impacted wisdom tooth and, once aboard, he could ride out on the helicopter and have the tooth extracted at the main base.

Because of the 120-mm mortars located in the Horseshoe and the antiaircraft guns which ringed the hill, the men on 881S had to employ a variety of diversions to keep the enemy gunners from getting the range of the incoming choppers. In this instance, they threw a smoke grenade a good distance away from the actual landing zone in hopes that the gunners would register on the smoke and the helicopter would be in and out before the North Vietnamese could readjust. This meant that the helo had about 19 seconds to get off the ground.

The ruse did not come off as planned. The stretcher bearers had

barely loaded the wounded man aboard the helicopter, a CH-46, when 120-mm mortar rounds bracketed the aircraft and spurred the pilot to action. The helo lurched into the air and the sudden jolt rolled the corporal with the bad tooth over the edge of the tail ramp; he held on desperately for a few seconds but finally let go and fell about 20 feet to the ground. Cursing to himself, the young man limped back to his trench and waited for another chance.

Later that day, a UH-34 swooped in to pick up another casualty and the prospective dental patient quickly scrambled aboard. This trip also covered about 20 feet — 10 feet up and 10 feet down — because the tail rotor of the UH-34 was literally sawed off by a burst from an enemy machine gun just after the bird became airborne. After the swirling craft came to rest, the passengers and the three-man crew quickly clambered out the hatch and dived into a nearby trench. A heavy mortar barrage ensued during which several more men were hit.

By the time another CH-46 arrived on the scene, the passenger list had grown to 14, including 10 casualties, the crew of the downed helo, and the original dental case. Because of the heavy concentration of enemy fire in the original zone, the Marines had blasted out another landing site on the opposite side of the hill. The chopper touched down and 13 of the 14 Marines boarded before the crew chief stated emphatically that the aircraft was full. As luck would have it, the young Marine with the swollen jaw was the 14th man. Thoroughly indignant, the three-time loser returned to his position and mumbled that he would rather suffer from a toothache than try and get off the hill by helicopter.

During the course of the battle, 881S became a small graveyard for helicopters; at least five were downed on or around the hill. Consequently, Company I gained a reputation among chopper crews which lasted long after the siege was over. When the 3d Battalion later departed Khe Sanh, Company I eventually moved to Hill 55 near Da Nang. One afternoon, while evacuating a wounded Marine, a CH-46 developed engine trouble and the pilot decided to shut down for repairs. Another flight was sent to pick up the wounded man and as the lead pilot approached he came up over the radio and asked his wingman where the landing zone was. The wingman replied: "Just look for the downed chopper, India (Company I) always marks their zones that way."

CH-47 Chinook

Big brother to the CH-46, the Chinook was strictly Army. Used for heavy transport missions, this helo was so widely used that some people think the "CH" designation common to all U.S. cargo helicopters stands for Chinook!

Manufacturer: Boeing Vertol
Crew: 3, plus 33 passengers
Dimensions: Rotor diameter: 59 ft.; Fuselage length: 51 ft.;
Height: 18 ft., 8 in.
Weight: 33,000 lbs. loaded
Speed: 190 mph max.
Armament: 1 7.62-mm machine gun
Service used by: US Army

The CH-47 Chinook helicopter was mainly used by the U.S. Army in Vietnam for transport of large, bulky items such as artillery and fuel bladders. Troop assault was also undertaken, sometimes using rope ladders to gain access to remote or difficult spots.

However, soldiers experimented with other uses of the Chinook. Examples are as an "ad hoc bomber" and a large armed gunship.

The Vietcong had developed tremendous underground fortifications and tunnel systems throughout Binh Dinh Province. Many of these fortifications could withstand almost any explosion. Riot agents were introduced to drive the enemy from his tunnels and force him into the open. During Operation PERSHING the 1st Cavalry dropped a total of 29,600 pounds of these agents from CH-47 aircraft using a simple locally fabricated fusing system on a standard drum. Initially the drums were merely rolled out the back of the open door of the Chinook and the fusing system was armed by a static line which permitted the drum to arm after it was free of the aircraft. Using this method, a large concentration of tear gas could be placed on a suspected area with accuracy.

Napalm was rigged and dropped in a similar manner during this same period. A single CH-47 could drop two and one-half tons of napalm on an enemy installation. Naturally, this method of dropping napalm was only used on specific targets where tactical air could not be effectively used.

Another version of the CH-47 which was unique to the 1st Cavalry

Division was the so-called "Go-Go Bird." The "Go-Go Bird," as it was called by the Infantry, was a heavily armed Chinook which the 1st Cavalry Division was asked to test in combat. Three test models were received armed with twin 20-mm Gatling guns, 40-mm grenade launchers, and .50-caliber machine guns, along with assorted ordnance. Though anything but graceful, it had a tremendous morale effect on the friendly troops which constantly asked for its support.

From the infantryman's viewpoint, when the "Go-Go Bird" came, the enemy disappeared.

Choppers Quiz

The helicopter used as a weapon and for transport came into its own during the Vietnam War. Adaptable for use everywhere in Indochina, the chopper was a common sight to U.S. Forces of all services as well as the American television audience following the war on the evening news.

Identify these choppers and correctly match them to their names. An extra choice is provided to confuse the issue.

1. _____ Bell OH-58 Kiowa

2. _____ Bell AH-1 Cobra

3. _____ Hughes OH-6 Cayuse ("Loach")

A

B

4. The standard rocket mounted on U.S. Army gunships or aerial rocket artillery helicopters was:

A. 1.75 inches in diameter
B. 2.75 "
C. 3.75 "
D. 4.75 "

FIGHTERS AND FIGHTER BOMBERS

All of the bombing of North Vietnam until late 1972 was carried out by fighter-bombers; the mammoth B-52's bombed the South in Arc Light strikes throughout the conflict, and were only used over North Vietnam in the last months. Strikes over the North were usually escorted by numerous fighters whose tasks were to fight off MIGs, jam radar, and attack antiaircraft gun and missile sites. Still, the often single-seat fighter-bombers and attack aircraft, whether launched from aircraft carriers or air bases in South Vietnam and Thailand, carried the burden of the war in North and South.

F-4 Phantom

The Phantom was first produced as a Navy and Marine carrier fighter; later the Air Force used it. Various models of the F-4 served the roles of interceptor, attack, and reconnaissance. USAF and USN Phantom crews shot down most of the MIGs destroyed.

Note: Specifications are for F-4B
Manufacturer: McDonnell Douglas
Crew: 2
Dimensions: Wingspan: 38 ft., 5 in.; Length: 58 ft., 4 in.;
Height: 16 ft., 3 in.
Weight: 44,600 lbs. loaded
Speed: 1,485 mph max.
Armament: 8 air-to-air missiles or 16,000 lb. bombs (USAF F-4E has 20-mm cannon)
Services used by: USAF, USMC, USN

It was a beautiful, sunny day in 1972. Lieutenant "Duke" Cunningham, pilot, and Lieutenant Junior Grade "Irish" Driscoll, radar intercept officer, were en route to the Hai Duong railroad yard in North Vietnam, in formation with 35 other Navy fighter and attack planes from the aircraft carrier *Constellation* (CV-64).

Their job, as flak suppressors, was to protect the slower moving light attack jets from antiaircraft artillery (AAA) and North Vietnamese MIG interceptors.

"For some reason the AAA was unusually quiet on this flight," Driscoll remembers. There were no enemy planes in sight either. So, they maneuvered high above Hai Duong while the A-7 *Corsairs* and A-6 *Intruders* dropped more than 30,000 pounds of bombs on the railroad facility. At some point during the attack, Cunningham swooped down and leveled a rail yard supply building with his *Rockeye.*

"As we pulled off the target four MIGs, which were a part of a larger group attacking the Navy planes, attacked us," says Cunningham. Their gunports were twinkling.

Cunningham veered left, maneuvered the F-4 *Phantom* behind one of the stubby, cigar-shaped MIGs and fired a heat-seeking *Sidewinder* missile. It blew off the tail and the enemy plane fell to the ground in flames.

"It happened in a matter of seconds," Driscoll says.

Careful to avoid the two pursuing MIGs, Cunningham flew into a steep vertical climb — a maneuver the trailing jets didn't follow. From higher altitude, Cunningham and Driscoll counted 22 attacking MIGs. Among them flew a surprised, but fighting Navy carrier attack force.

"The sky was real busy," Cunningham remembers.

In their more than 150 combat missions together, while assigned to the *Fighting Falcons* of VF-96 Cunningham and Driscoll had never witnessed such a large North Vietnamese air attack — especially over Hai Duong. Since the beginning of the war, Hai Duong had been a frequent target for U.S. Navy and Air Force bombers which, except for heavy antiaircraft fire, pounded it unopposed. In fact, the size of this particular enemy air attack was so unexpected that many Navy aircrews initially thought the MIGs were U.S. Air Force planes flying in to assist the Navy raid.

Worried about their fellow aviators, Cunningham and Driscoll flew down into the melee. They skillfully maneuvered behind another MIG and squeezed off a second heat-seeking missile.

"The guy didn't even know we were behind him," says Cunningham.

Adds Driscoll, "The missile went straight up his tailpipe and exploded. The MIG burst into a bright red fireball."

By now, the sky was inundated with heavy machine gun fire and surface-to-air missiles (SAMs) from North Vietnamese antiaircraft batteries on the ground. The carrier aircraft, which had lost one plane to antiaircraft fire and shot down four MIGs, were in the process of returing to *Constellation*. All payloads had been dropped. The Hai Duong railroad yard was ablaze.

Cunningham turned the *Phantom* toward the Gulf of Tonkin, but a MIG-17 suddenly appeared ahead of them. It zipped by, gunports flashing. Cunningham pulled the *Phantom* into a 90-degree vertical climb. But, to his surprise, the MIG pilot copied the maneuver and eventually fell in behind the *Phantom*.

"We tried shaking him off our tail, but no matter what we did he stayed with us," says Driscoll. "That pilot really knew how to fly his airplane."

Later, Cunningham and Driscoll learned the MIG pilot was Colonel Toon, reputed to be North Vietnam's leading ace with 13 American kills to his credit.

After three minutes of fast high-G maneuvering and steep vertical climbs, Toon (who Cunningham and Driscoll guessed was running low on fuel) broke off his attack and attempted to flee.

"That was his mistake," says Driscoll, "because as he pulled away, we turned, put our nose on his tail and fired another heat-seeking missile."

The missile detonated just beyond the tail. Toon's plane hit the ground and exploded.

Cunningham pointed the *Phantom* toward *Constellation*, then stationed 100 miles offshore. But, the lengthy five-minute dogfight (most lasted between 30 to 45 seconds) had taken them miles inland over enemy territory and more surface-to-air missile batteries. Minutes after destroying Toon's plane, Cunningham noticed several SAMs flying up towards them. They managed to avoid a couple of them before one finally hit the *Phantom*. The jet shook violently and began to spin.

"I was never more afraid of anything in my life," says Cunningham. "The plastic bubble I had put around myself, which I felt was invincible, was shattered. My biggest fear was realized and I thought Willie and I were going to be prisoners of war."

The *Phantom* suffered massive hydraulic failure and its wing was aflame.

Cunningham nursed it as far as he could over the Gulf of Tonkin. When he was no longer able to control the jet, both aviators ejected and parachuted into the water, very close to the shore.

As they descended, Cunningham and Driscoll saw several North Vietnamese PT boats speeding out of Haiphong Harbor after them. Cunningham immediately called for help on his survival radio. Within minutes, several Navy aircraft appeared, sank one of the PT boats and strafed the others until a U.S. Marine Corps helicopter from USS *Okinawa* (LPH-3) retrieved them 15 minutes later. They were taken safely aboard *Okinawa*. The ordeal was over.

On May 10, 1972, Cunningham and Driscoll (who together shot down a MIG on January 19 and another on May 8) celebrated a total of five enemy kills, the number needed to qualify as an ace. They also earned the distinction of becoming the first aces of the Vietnam war; first F-4 *Phantom* aces; first aviators to destroy three MIGs in one aerial battle; and the first all-missile aces (meaning all adversaries were shot down by *Sidewinder* missiles).

F-8 Crusader

Vought's F-8 was an early supersonic carrier fighter, which was pressed into bombing service in the early war years, since it could operate off smaller carriers than some of the larger multi-purpose airplanes.

Manufacturer: LTV
Crew: 1
Dimensions: Wingspan: 35 ft., 2 in.; Length: 54 ft., 6 in.; Height: 15 ft., 9 in.
Weight loaded: 28,000 lbs.
Speed: 1,135 mph
Armament: 4 20-mm cannon; Rockets and bombs
Service used by: USN

Loss of oil pressure, probably due to failure of No. 6 engine bearing, required an F-8 pilot to head for his in-country bingo field. Seventy-five miles out the engine began to vibrate, there were three explosions from the rear of the aircraft and the engine started to unwind. The pilot countered this by pushing the throttle forward. He noted some engine response and then called his wingman to report the explosions. The wingman told him his plane was on fire and advised him to eject.

The pilot positioned himself erect in the seat, placed his feet on the rudder pedals and pulled the face curtain. The aircraft was 25 miles off the coast, 7500 feet altitude, wings level and in a descent of about 2000 feet per minute at 270 knots.

"I was conscious of the upward acceleration of the seat," he recalls. "As I cleared the aircraft the face curtain slipped to the side into the

air stream and I could see that I was tumbling forward. There was a tug on the straps, followed by a second harder tug. I then found myself floating in my parachute."

He inflated his LPA-1, removed his oxygen mask and let it hang, still attached to the seat pan. He released his seat pack and the raft fell below him and inflated. He waved at his orbiting wingman to signal that he was OK.

"At 3000 feet altitude," he continues, "I spotted a sampan on the water below me. It looked as if I was going to land close to it and I became concerned that the occupants might be unfriendly. I took my survival radio from my survival vest and tried to contact my wingman, first on guard and then SAR common frequency but got no answer. Although I was getting good side tones and I could hear the guard beeper transmitting, I learned after that neither the cover aircraft nor the rescue aircraft picked up any of my transmissions. Finally I broadcast several times in the blind that I had just ejected, was in good condition and was about to land near a sampan. I put the radio on beeper and put it back into my vest. Then, considering that my wingman overhead obviously had me in sight and in the interest of conserving radio battery, I turned it off.

"As I got to about 1000 or 500 feet over the water, I sensed the downward relative motion and my raft started to swing erratically below me. I put my hands on the risers (I was not wearing gloves) and felt for the koch fittings. When I saw the raft hit the water I straightened my legs and pointed my toes. I released the koch fittings as my feet hit, went under and bobbed right back to the surface. The parachute floated well clear out ahead of me. I easily separated myself from the chute. I saw my raft floating about 25 feet away, swam to it, pulled myself in, belly down, rolled over and sat up. I noticed a yellow substance in the water which may have been dye marker although I had not used the marker attached to my torso harness.

"I landed about a half-mile away from the sampan, which started heading in my direction after I landed. I considered taking out my pistol but instead I pulled out my radio and took off my helmet. I still couldn't contact anyone so I put the radio back in my vest. While I sat in the raft my wingman made a few low passes over me and I waved my arms to signal I was OK.

"The sampan approached and pulled up alongside my raft. Three or four men were standing forward and a woman and two children were standing aft. An elderly man motioned several times for me to get into the boat and pointed to a heater or stove. He seemed to be trying to say that I could dry off or that they had food for me. I made several gestures with my arms indicating that I wanted to stay in the raft and that they should go away. My wingman flew over us at low altitude about that time. Apparently they understood my gestures because the sampan circled the raft once and then went off about three-quarters of a mile and remained there throughout the helicopter pickup. At no time did they take any hostile action.

"By now I could see an A-3 Skywarrior circling overhead and the mast of another boat out on the horizon. I found the lanyard tied to the raft and pulled in the seat pack which I was about to open when I heard a motor. Immediately I thought of the boat I had seen on the horizon and envisioned an enemy or unfriendly motor launch outbound to pick me up. I put the seat pack back over the side and swung the raft around 360 degrees but everything seemed the same as before. The motor noise went away so I sat and waited. After a couple of minutes I heard the motor again but this time it sounded like a helicopter rotor.

"I swung the raft around once more and sighted the helo about three miles off. I pulled in the seat pack again, opened it, cut off a smoke flare with my shroud cutter and lit the day end. Apparently the helo crew sighted it because they started toward me. The flare burned out and the helo stopped about a mile away so I lit off a second smoke flare. The helo then flew over me, orbited, returned and hovered. I put my helmet back on, rolled out of the raft and immediately became entangled with some underwater lines. Then I realized that I had not released my hip rocket jet fittings. I released these and my oxygen mask and swam about 30 feet away from the raft. A crewman in a bathing suit jumped from the helo into the water and the helo made another orbit.

"The crewman swam over to me and asked if I was injured. I told him that I was all right and floated in my life vest while he felt my arms and legs to make sure there were no broken bones. The helo returned and dropped something nearby (possibly a smoke flare), made one more orbit, then hovered some distance away and dropped a three-pronged rescue seat. The crewman pulled me over to the rescue seat and helped me onto it. Rotor wash from the helo was blowing water in my face so I put my helmet visor down. The crewman strapped me onto the seat and I was hoisted up and pulled into the helo. The helo made another orbit during which time I think the crewman sank my raft. He was then hoisted aboard and I was flown to the bingo field without incident. The only after-effects I had were a sore back between my shoulder blades and a stiff neck, both of which went away in a couple of days."

F-100 Super Sabre

First of the Air Force's "Century Series", the F-100 evolved from a long line of North American fighters beginning with World War II's P-51 Mustang. The first Super Sabres went to Vietnam painted silver overall; experience soon dictated camouflage paint to render it and other US aircraft less conspicuous.

Manufacturer: North American Rockwell
Crew: 1
Dimensions: Wingspan: 38 ft., 9 in.; Length: 47 ft.,
Height: 16 ft., 3 in.
Weight: 30,000 lbs. loaded
Speed: 864 mph max.
Armament: 4 20-mm cannon; 7,500 lb. bombs
Service used by: USAF

Enlisting in the Marine Corps in 1942, George E. Day served 30 months in the South Pacific during World War II. Commissioned in the Air National Guard in 1950, the 26-year-old was called to active duty to begin pilot training in 1951.

He served two tours as a fighter-bomber pilot in the Far East during the Korean War. In a later assignment to England, George became the first pilot to survive a "no-parachute" bailout from a burning jet fighter.

In Vietnam, Day was the first commander of the F-100 fighter squadron that flew high-speed forward-air-control missions in areas where the slow-moving FAC birds could not survive hostile groundfire.

On August 26, 1967, Major Day was airborne over North Vietnam on a forward air control mission when his F-100 was hit by enemy groundfire. During ejection from the stricken fighter his right arm was broken in three places and his left knee was badly sprained. He was immediately captured by the North Vietnamese and taken to a prison camp.

Continually interrogated and tortured, his injuries were neglected for two days until a medic crudely set his broken arm. Despite the pain of torture, he steadfastly refused to give any information to his captors.

On September 1, feigning a severe back injury, George lulled his guards into relaxing their vigil and slipped out of his ropes to escape into the jungle. During the trek south toward the demilitarized zone, he evaded enemy patrols and survived on a diet of berries and uncooked frogs. On the second night a bomb or rocket detonated nearby, and Major Day was hit in the right leg by the shrapnel. He was bleeding from the nose and ears due to the shock effect of the explosion. To rest and recover from these wounds, George hid in the jungle for two days.

Continuing the nightmarish journey, he met barrages from American artillery as he neared the Ben Hai River, which separated North Vietnam from South Vietnam. With the aid of a float made from a bamboo log, he swam across the river and entered the no man's land called the demilitarized zone. Delirious and disoriented from his injuries, George wandered aimlessly for several days, trying frantically to signal US aircraft. He was not spotted by two FAC pilots who flew directly overhead, and, later, George limped toward two Marine helicopters only to arrive at the landing zone just after the choppers pulled away.

Single-seat F-100 in natural metal finish. Later F-100s were painted in a multicolor jungle camouflage scheme.

Twelve days after the escape, weakened from exposure, hunger, and his wounds, Major Day was ambushed and captured by the Vietcong. He suffered gunshot wounds to his left hand and thigh while trying to elude his pursuers. George was returned to the original prison camp and brutally punished for his escape attempt.

On a starvation diet, the 170-pound man shrank to 110 pounds. He was refused medical treatment for broken bones, gunshot wounds, and infections. Renewing the pressure to force Major Day to give vital military information, the North Vietnamese beat and tortured him for two days. Finally, he was bound by a rope under his armpits and suspended from a ceiling beam for over two hours until the interrogating officer ordered a guard to twist his mangled right arm, breaking George's wrist.

Two months after his Super Sabre had been shot down, Major Day was transferred to a prison camp near the capital city of Hanoi. By this time he was totally incapacitated, with infections in his arms and legs and little feeling in his twisted hands. George could not perform even the simplest tasks for himself, but still was tortured.

After five and one-half years of captivity, George E. Day was released on March 14, 1973.

F-105 Thunderchief

The first single-seat supersonic aircraft capable of carrying a nuclear bomb, the F-105 was powerful and fast at low altitude. 105's flew many missions over the North, with a high loss rate. A conspicuous mountainous area near Hanoi was dubbed "Thud Ridge" in the plane's honor. Two-seat F-105F's carried out Wild Weasel flak-suppression missions.

Note: Specifications are for F-105F Wild Weasel version
Unofficial name: Thud
Manufacturer: Fairchild Republic
Crew: 2
Dimensions: Wingspan: 34 ft., 11 in.; Length: 69 ft., 1 in.; Height: 10 ft., 2 in.
Weight: 40,000 lbs. loaded
Speed: 1,390 mph
Armament: 1 20-mm cannon; 14,000 lb. bombs, rockets
Service used by: USAF

On April 19, 1967, Major Leo K. Thorsness and his back-seater, Captain Harold E. Johnson, were nearing the 100-mission mark that would bring their combat tour to an end.

Leo was the "old head" weasel pilot at Takhli and the instructor for newly assigned crews. MIGs had chased Leo and Harry through the skies of North Vietnam, and the experienced pair had evaded 53 SAMs. Describing the flak-and-SAM-suppression missions, Leo said, "In essence, we would go in high enough to let somebody shoot at us and low enough to go down and get them; then we went in and got them." The weasels would be the first flight on target, preceding the main attack and remaining after the strike force had departed. It was like trolling for sharks in a canoe!

Leo led his flight of four Thuds from the tanker in southern Laos toward the North Vietnamese border. They were headed for the Xuan Mai army barracks and storage supply area 30 miles to the southwest of Hanoi. Xuan Mai lay on the edge of the Red River delta, where rice paddies give way to forested mountains. Hopefully, the defenses would not be as lethal as those ringing downtown Hanoi.

The rattlesnake tone in Leo's headset buzzed in time with the flickering strobes on Harry's scope. The eerie sound signalled that already the enemy missile crews were warming up the SAM radars and searching for American aircraft. The rattlesnake whined louder and the strobes got bigger as the weasels flew deeper into North Vietnam.

Though the bear's warning gear detected the SAM tracking and guidance radars, the weasel crews had no guaranteed cockpit indication of a launch. If they were lucky, they would spot the lethal "telephone pole" rising from its pad in a cloud of dust. If they were not so lucky, they would find the missile while there was still time to avoid it with a desperation maneuver. If their luck had run out, the missile would streak in undetected from behind, and its high-explosive warhead would shatter the unsuspecting Thunderchief.

Leo sent his number 3 and 4 men to the north of Xuan Mai as he and number 2 headed to the south. Now the enemy gunners would be forced to divide their attention between the separated flights.

Major Thorsness maneuvered toward a strong SAM signal and fired a radar-seeking Shrike missile. The site was seven miles distant and obscured by haze, so Leo and Harry never saw the missile hit. But the abrupt disappearance of the enemy's signal from Harry's scope indicated that the Shrike had probably done its job.

Leo picked up a second SAM site visually and rolled into a diving attack through a curtain of AAA fire. He pickled his CBUs (cluster bomb units) dead on target and pulled out of the steep dive.

The two Thuds accelerated toward the treetops where they would have the best chance for survival. But number 2 was in trouble. Anti-aircraft rounds had found Tom Madison's machine, and the glowing overheat light confirmed that his engine had been hit. Leo told Tom to head for the hills to the west, but the rescue beeper on guard (emergency) radio channel signalled that Madison and his back-seater, Tom Sterling, had already bailed out. Somehow Leo found time in the midst of the emergency to fire another Shrike at a third SAM site.

To the north numbers 3 and 4 had survived an air battle with MIG interceptors. Number 3's afterburner would not light, and without

the added thrust the flight could not sustain the supersonic speed to outrun their attackers. Somehow 3 and 4 staved off two more MIGs as they limped south toward Takhli. Leo's Thud was now the only fighter-bomber in the Xuan Mai area.

Major Thorsness circled the descending parachutes while Harry relayed information to "Crown," the rescue control aircraft. Suddenly Harry spotted a MIG off their left wing, and Leo recalls, "I wasn't sure whether or not he was going to attack the parachutes. So I said, 'Why not?' and took off after him. I was a little high, dropped down to 1,000 feet and headed north behind him. I was driving right up his tailpipe at 550 knots. At about 3,000 feet I opened up on him with the 20 millimeter but completely missed him. We attacked again, and I was pulling and holding the trigger when Harry got my attention with the MIGs behind us. If I had hit that MIG good, we would have swallowed some of the explosion (debris). But we got him."

Low on gas, Leo sped south toward the tanker, following the progress of the rescue forces on his radio. The prop-driven Sandys that would direct the on-scene effort and the rescue helicopters that would attempt the pick-up were already headed toward the downed weasel crew.

With full tanks but with only 500 rounds of ammunition, Leo left the tanker and flew north again. While briefing the Sandy pilots on the defenses around Xuan Mai, he spotted three interceptors ahead. "One of the MIGs flew right into my gunsight at about 2,000 feet and pieces started falling off the (enemy) aircraft. They hadn't seen us, but they did now."

Harry warned that four MIGs were closing from the rear and Leo dove for the deck, eluding his pursuers as the Thud raced through the mountain passes with the afterburner blazing.

Now the MIGs turned back toward the slow-moving Sandys and Thorsness radioed a warning, "Okay, Sandy One. Just keep that machine of yours turning and they can't get you." Low on fuel again and without ammunition, Leo turned toward the MIGs with one idea in mind: "To try to get them on me." He knew the Sandys would be sitting ducks for the MIGs.

At last a flight of 105s arrived, and now the MIGs were on the defensive. By evening, the Americans claimed the MIG that Leo had killed plus four probables, including the enemy aircraft that had flown in front of Leo's deadly guns.

The 1,000-foot flames and billowing smoke from Xuan Mai could be seen over 40 miles away — a silent testimony to the success of the airstrike.

Fighters & Fighter Bombers Quiz

1. This USAF F-4C Phantom II is:

A. Launching rockets against a ground target somewhere in South Vietnam
B. Laying a smoke screen to obscure following aircraft from North Vietnamese radar screens
C. Dumping fuel prior to making an emergency landing at a base in Southeast Asia
D. Dropping marker bombs to pinpoint targets for following aircraft

2. The F-4 Phantom, used as a bomber and fighter by the Air Force, Navy, and Marines, was armed only with missiles, unlike older fighters with 20 mm. cannons. This proved:

A. So successful against enemy aircraft that cannons were replaced with missiles on the other aircraft types
B. Useless in close-range dogfighting. Later the Phantoms were equipped with 20 mm. Vulcan cannons in a pod or in a completely redesigned nose
C. Neither more or less effective than the cannons in the older aircraft

3. Identify this USN aircraft:

A. Douglas A-1 Skyraider (or Spad or Sandy)
B. Lockheed WV-2 (Air Force designation: EC-121) Constellation
C. LTV F8U or F-8A Crusader

BOMBERS AND ATTACK PLANES

Rugged, low-flying, slow, heavily armored, and undefended against enemy fighters, attack planes were designed strictly for ground attack, and not as multi-purpose fighter-bombers with an interceptor capability. Whether operating from aircraft carriers or ground bases, these mostly single-engine planes bore much of the brunt of the air war over North and South. The "attack" designation was first used by the Navy, and later adopted by the Air Force.

B-52 Stratofortress

The huge B-52, still in our first-line of defense today after 30 years of service, was produced as a long-range nuclear bomber for Strategic Air Command. For Vietnam service, they flew from Guam, loaded with conventional "iron" bombs on modified internal and external racks. In 1972, they finally bombed the North during the misnamed "Christmas bombing" and were even credited with shooting down attacking MIG fighters.

Note: Specifications are for B-52D
Manufacturer: Boeing
Unofficial name: BUFF (Big Ugly Flying "Fellow")
Crew: 6
Dimensions: Wingspan: 185 ft.; Length: 156 ft., 7 in.;
Height: 48 ft., 4 in.
Weight: 450,000 lbs. loaded
Speed: 630 mph max.
Armament: 4 50-cal. machine guns in tail turret; 60,000 lb. bombs
Service using: USAF

For the first time in the air war, gunners aboard B-52 bombers accounted for five MIG-21 kills.*

The first victory credited to a gunner came on the night of December

*During the Korean War, there were 27 victories recorded by B-29 gunners.

18, 1972. Staff Sergeant Samuel O. Turner, normally stationed at March AFB, California, but on temporary duty with the 307th Strategic Wing based at U-Tapao airfield, Thailand, was the tail gunner aboard a B-52D, part of the heavy bomber force hitting targets in the Hanoi area. Turner describes the engagement:

"We were a few ships back from the lead aircraft. As we approached our target area, numerous surface-to-air missiles began coming up and exploding around us.

As we drew nearer to the target the intensity of the SAM's picked up. They were lighting up the sky. They seemed to be everywhere. We released our bombs over the target and had just proceeded outbound from the target when we learned that there were MIG aircraft airborne near a particular reference point.

Our navigator told us the reference point was in our area and before long we learned the enemy fighter had us on its radar. As he closed on us I also picked him up on my radar when he was a few miles from our aircraft.

A few seconds later, the fighter locked on to us. As the MIG closed in, I also locked on him. He came in low in a rapid climb. While tracking the first MIG, I picked up a second enemy aircraft at 8 o'clock at a range of about 7½ miles. He appeared stabilized — not attacking us, obviously allowing the other fighter room to maneuver and conduct his run first.

As the attacking MIG came into firing range, I fired a burst. There was a gigantic explosion to the rear of the aircraft. I looked out the window but was unable to see directly where the MIG would have been. I looked back at my radar scope. Except for the one airplane out at 8 o'clock, there was nothing. And within 15 seconds, even he broke away and we lost contact with him."

Turner's MIG kill was witnessed by another gunner, Master Sergeant Lewis E. LeBlanc, who confirmed the kill. LeBlanc saw a fireball at the MIG-21's approximate range and azimuth.

Airman First Class Albert E. Moore, a B-52 gunner, won credit for the next MIG. A tail gunner during a bombing raid on the Thai Nguyen railroad yards on December 24, he acquired a fast-moving bogey on his radar scope. He notified his crew to dispense chaff and flares, got target lock-on at 4,000 yards, and as the bandit closed to 2,000 yards, opened fire. He continued firing until the blip blossomed on his scope, then disappeared. His feat was witnessed by T/Sgt. Clarence W. Chute, also a gunner, who saw the MIG-21 "on fire and falling away."

When several flights of B-52s worked over a target, the results were awesome. The exploding bombs churned up strips of the terrain several thousand meters long and the ground for miles around literally shook from the blasts. Many enemy casualties were sustained from the concussion alone. One entry from a captured North Vietnamese diary read: "18 February: The heavy bombing of the jets and B-52 explosions are so strong that our lungs hurt." In some instances, NVA soldiers were found after a strike wandering around in a daze with blood streaming from their noses and mouths. Often the internal hemorrhaging induced by the concussion was so severe that it resulted in death. Quite understandably, such missions could not be unleashed too close to the Marines.

A-1 Skyraider

The A-1 Skyraider was designed at the end of World War II as a powerful prop-driven Navy carrier attack aircraft. Called "Spad" because it was so old, the A-1 flew over North and South, most notably as escort for rescue missions, blasting those who would attempt to capture our men.

Manufacturer: Douglas
Former Navy designation: AD
Crew: 1 (A-1H); 2 (A-1E and G)
Dimensions: Wingspan: 50 ft.; Length: 39 ft., 3 in.;
Height: 15 ft., 10 in.
Weight: 18,000 lbs. loaded
Speed: 365 mph max.
Armament: 4 20-mm cannon, 8,000 lb. bombs, rockets max.
Services using: USN, USAF, VNAF

Korean War vintage, propeller-driven A-1 Skyraiders, like the helicopters they escorted on rescue missions, were slow and faced extreme danger when flying into an area where enemy defenses could shoot down a modern jet fighter.

Rescue was indeed a risky business, and A-1 pilots shared the danger with the chopper crews. By 1967 the A-1E had the highest overall loss rate of any airplane in Southeast Asia. Skyraider loss rates per 1,000 sorties ranged from 1.0 in South Vietnam to 2.3 over Laos and up to 6.2 for missions over North Vietnam. The high loss rate over North Vietnam was directly attributable to the A-1's rescue escort role. Of the twenty-five A-1s shot down over North Vietnam between June 1966 and June 1967, seven were lost on rescue missions.

Planning, skill, tactics, and equipment, combined with raw courage, pulled rescue forces through the most precarious situations. Death or captivity, however, were always possibilities.

All these elements were present during a rescue effort that began on November 5, 1965, when an F-105, returning from a mission near Hanoi, flew into a cloud and disappeared. The wingman reported the F-105's last known position, but noticed no antiaircraft fire, missile firings, or explosion. Because of the rapidly deteriorating weather and approaching darkness no rescue attempt was made.

At dawn, under clearing skies, Sandy 11 and Sandy 12, a pair of A-1s, flew over North Vietnam to where the F-105 had disappeared. Antiaircraft fire hit Sandy 12, and the pilot ejected. Sandy 11 circled

U.S. Navy Skyraider prepares for catapult launch off an aircraft carrier.

and soon spotted the downed pilot. Jolly Green 85, a CH-3C com-
manded by Capt. Warren R. Lilly, was enroute to the survivor as two
more A-1Es scrambled from Udorn to form a search and rescue task
force. Enemy small arms fire cut into Jolly 85 as it neared the survivor.
Lilly managed to raise his badly damaged helicopter to an altitude
sufficient for bailing out. As the Sandys circled, Lilly punched in the
automatic pilot and made his way to the door. Pilots in the A-1s
reported that four chutes had opened and soon made voice and
beeper contact with the downed crewmen.

A U.S. Navy Sikorsky SH-3 Sea Knight helicopter, reported it was
flying toward the crash scene from the carrier *Independence*. Two A-1Es,
Sandys 13 and 14, flew to intercept the Sea Knight and escort it into

the rescue area. They rendezvoused with it just east of the Vietnamese coast and flew alongside over the beach and westward toward the jungled mountains of North Vietnam. When the pilot of Sandy 14 spotted 37-mm tracers he peeled off into a cloud in an evasive maneuver. Like the F-105, Sandy 14 disappeared forever.

At dusk, just before abandoning the search until dawn, a Navy A-1 pilot monitored a beeper's signal. As darkness engulfed the circling task force, the SH-3 helicopter dipped down for a tree-top level visual search. The copilot spotted a tiny light and ordered the penetrator down to pick up the parajumper from Jolly Green 85. The A-1Es and the helicopter, with an Air Force sergeant — who would be forever grateful to the U.S. Navy and his Zippo cigarette lighter — safely aboard, returned to the *Independence.*

The next morning, encouraged by the rescue of the parajumper, the search for other survivors of Jolly Green 85 continued.

A-1s flew low over the helicopter wreckage and finally picked up the sound of a beeper. Two Air Force Skyraider pilots were concentrating on the signal when enemy gunfire ripped, almost simultaneously, into both airplanes. While the two damaged A-1s returned to Udorn, their comrades strafed the enemy gunners who answered with 23-mm, 37-mm, and small arms fire. Meanwhile, rescue controllers in Saigon and at the rescue control centers at Udorn and Da Nang decided that further efforts would only result in additional casualties.

Their decision, though a painful one, was correct. Captain Warren Lilly, Lieutenant Jerry Singleton, and Staff Sergeant Arthur Cromier, captured soon after parachuting into the jungle, were already miles away, on their way to prison camps in Hanoi.

A-4 Skyhawk

Ed Heinemann, who also designed the A-1 and other capable warplanes, gave the Skyhawk small delta wings to eliminate the need for folding wings aboard Navy carriers. The "bantam" or "tinkertoy bomber" flew many missions over North and South in Navy and Marine markings, and once even shot down a MIG!

Manufacturer: Douglas
Former Navy designation: A4D
Crew: 1
Dimensions: Wingspan: 27 ft., 6 in.; Length: 40 ft.;
Height: 15 ft.
Weight: 18,000 lbs. loaded
Speed: 675 mph max.
Armament: 2 20-mm cannon, 8,000 lbs. ordnance max.
Services using: USN, USMC

A special quality of the A-4 is its ability to take great punishment and still remain airborne. Admiring pilots believe the Skyhawk's stubborn desire to keep flying saved many of them from a dunking in the ocean or "a visit to the Hanoi Hilton."

During a strike over North Vietnam, a Skyhawk being piloted by Lieutenant junior grade Al Crebo was hit by ground fire; the plane's rudder went out and it began to burn from the base of the wings outward. Despite the serious damage, Crebo flew the burning jet to the relative safety of the Gulf of Tonkin before he bailed out near an aircraft carrier. He was soon rescued from the Gulf waters.

Such determination by the little A-4 is not uncommon. USS *Hancock* aviators like to tell of the time a pilot flew his Skyhawk back from a strike deep in North Vietnam and made an uneventful arrested landing aboard the ship. The plane was riddled with 34 flak holes.

Lieutenant Hart ("Irish") Schwarzenbach told of the close call he had while flying a combat mission over Vinh: "We were hitting a well-defended target and I was flying as the fourth man in the slot. Right after my roll-in, my plane was hit in the left wing; it inverted completely. All I could think about was the downtown dance in Vinh and how I was going to be a participant.

"It took a bit of strain to right the plane, but the Skyhawk was still up there and would not give in. I could see from the reflection on the ground that I was streaming a trail of fuel, making me a good target. An A-3 Skywarrior tanker picked me up at the coastline and pumped fuel to the engine all the way to the ship where, even with a hole blasted in the wing, I made a nice, easy landing."

Besides its ability to remain airborne, the Skyhawk has other good combat qualities. Because of its small size and light weight, it makes sharper turns and comes out of dives faster.

The Skyhawk's maneuverability was praised by Lieutenant Commander T.R. Swartz, credited with a MIG kill.

The kill was recorded May 1, 1967, during an attack on the North Vietnamese airfield at Kep. Swartz had just fired several of his rockets at two MIG's on the runway when he got a radio call telling him there were two MIG's at his "six o'clock position" (on his tail).

"I spotted the attacking aircraft and put my A-4 into a high barrel roll, dropping in behind the MIG's," Swartz recalls. "From this markedly advantageous position, I fired several air-to-ground rockets at the number two MIG and then got another call that there was a MIG at my six o'clock again. I was not able to see my rockets hit as I bent my A-4 hard, checking for the suspected third MIG."

Swartz's wingman confirmed a MIG kill; he saw the enemy aircraft hit the ground.

Another advantage of the Skyhawk is the visibility it permits the pilot. There are no line-of-sight restrictions from wings or hoods. Skyhawk pilots consider canopy visibility so good it's almost like riding in a convertible car. This lack of interference with a pilot's view of his surroundings is of great importance in terms of his survival.

Lieutenant junior grade Roger Van Dyke expressed an opinion common to his fellow A-4 pilots: "The A-4 is only 40 feet long and has a wing spread of less than 30 feet, but its weapon delivery system, its speed, its maneuverability and its determination to stay in the air under adverse circumstances — coupled with a pilot's own determination — [was] a great combination for combat flying in Vietnam."

This Navy enlisted man is fusing a 500-lb. bomb under the wing of an attack plane aboard USS *America* (CVA-66).

Big, slow, and heavily laden A-6s flew at night and through all kinds of weather. Since North Vietnam was often shrouded by clouds and fog, the Intruder's radar and electronics located targets few other planes could.

Manufacturer: Grumman
Crew: 2
Dimensions: Wingspan: 53 ft.; Length: 54 ft., 7 in.;
Height: 16 ft.
Weight: 60,000 lbs. fully loaded
Speed: 685 mph max.
Armament: 18,000 lb. bombs
Services using: USN, USMC

A-6 Intruder

Some cannot accept danger and are forced to ignore it or run away from it. They are in trouble. I get diarrhea, but I get back from my missions.

The mission I am about to describe is one I actually flew. It is not typical of air strikes in North Vietnam, but it is typical if you happen to fly the A-6 Intruder. I cannot, of course, describe tactics in detail, since I may wish to use them again. I believe you may, however, get a feeling for the factors that affect a pilot's nerves. The target, which shall remain nameless, is one of the most heavily defended in the world — scores of automatic weapons and anti-aircraft batteries and a few surface-to-air missiles.

The ride to the flight deck is via the same sort of elevator you might find in an office building back home. The usual elevator small talk is tossed around and perhaps there is a last-minute instruction or agreement between members of a crew.

As we step out onto the flight deck, a misty rain driven by 34 mph winds cools our faces and begins to dampen our clothing. The deck is lighted by an eerie moonglow of red lights, but beyond that there is only the pitch-black darkness of a night conjured up by the devil especially for carrier-based aviators. Our aircraft, laden with more than 20 500-lb. bombs, presents a silhouette which immediately sets aside any comparisons I might make between this mission and the hundreds of training flights that were intended to prepare me for it.

I am greeted by the plane captain, a young man with a grueling job. This is his airplane. When it's aboard ship, he lives with it — cleans it, inspects it, polishes it, inspects it again and sleeps with it. He is justifiably proud of the plane and of himself. When we get it airborne, he'll take a well-deserved break, but I'm sure he'll stop long enough to say a prayer for us.

As I walk around the aircraft for preflight inspection, the ordnancemen are completing the fusing of the bombs. All four A-6's on this launch have been loaded within the past hour with the same bomb load as mine — more than 80 500's, all loaded by hand by ten men. Like the plane captain, the ordnancemen work from 14 to 20 hours a day and, like you and me, they get tired.

When at last I climb into the cockpit, my bombardier/navigator is already strapped in and is busily aligning his inertial platform. He's Lieutenant junior grade Bruce Borchers, and, as you will see, he's easily the coolest man in the world. The training of these men parallels that of the pilot but emphasizes technology. The weapon system belongs to them. Although some say a monkey could run an A-6 system as long as everything works, when a component fails, immediate response by a highly skilled operator is required to complete the mission.

With almost no time for thought, the engines are running, the system is checked out and we're taxiing onto the catapult. Troubleshooters give us a careful check and the catapult officer is waving his green wand back and forth in a slow, rhythmic movement. "Takeoff check list complete. All set?"

I switch the external lights on and wait. The green wand moves slowly down until it touches the deck. We are slammed back against the seat until the aircraft has accelerated from zero to 140 mph, into a huge wet ink bottle. "Wheels up and we're climbing . . . 170, flaps up . . . looks good."

It's all business and no time to think. System updated and checked out. Airplane's in good shape. Coast-in in five minutes. There's an entire fleet out here just so we can get those bombs on the target. Everything we miss will move further south tomorrow — that much closer to the Marines.

Coast-in. Bruce says calmly, "Feet dry." "Rodge." The enemy knows we're here and he's tracking us, but he can't lay anything on us . . . yet. My throat is awfully dry as I bank hard toward the target. I wish for 800 knots. There's Bruce again: "I have the target." Suddenly the sky lights up like daylight. "Roger, target." I glance at him. His features are clear in the flickering light of anti-aircraft artillery. Believe me, his expression is blank — pure concentration on the radar scope. "In attack." He sounds as though he's on a training mission. "Roger in attack in range. Committed. Let's make it a good one, Babe."

As we approach the target, the flak gets more intense. Suddenly, this monster I'm herding around begins to shudder and shake like a toy in a storm. The 85's are on us, but there's just a second to go to release. Bombs away, and I break out so hard we nearly stall. They're not so close now, but still shooting. "Which way out?" I glance at Bruce. He's quietly typing away on his computer keyboard, as a bright orange glow from our bombs illuminates the cockpit. The run is over. "Take steering."

Named in honor of Vought's famous WW II fighter bomber, the A-7 was based on the proven design of the F-8 Crusader. Unlike its older sibling, the A-7 was subsonic and carried a large bomb load. Intended as a follow-on for the A-4, the A-7 was flown by both Navy and Air Force pilots.

Manufacturer: LTV
Unofficial name: SLUF (Short Little Ugly "Fellow")
Crew: 1
Dimensions: Wingspan: 38 ft., 9 in.; Length: 46 ft., 1 in.;
Height: 16 ft., 2 in.
Weight: 42,000 lbs. fully loaded
Speed: 580 mph max.
Armament: 1 20-mm cannon, 15,000 lb. bombs
Services using: USN, USAF

A-7 Corsair II

In the spring of 1975, Air Force A-7Ds and Navy A-7Es were among the last U.S. aircraft to fly combat missions in Southeast Asia when they supported the helicopter evacuations of Saigon. The leader of one flight of these USAF A-7s describes his feelings during the final hours.

"Now 'Cricket' (the Airborne Command and Control C-130) was calling me: 'Karen lead, rendezvous with the choppers at Point Hope and provide escort.' Night helicopter escort at low level! Well, we'd never done it before, but then we'd never evacuated Saigon before, either. Besides, the adrenalin level was now so high, it was hard to think of caution. Invulnerability is a heady thing.

"It was pitch black now, and over Point Hope we could see nothing. The Marine chopper pilots realized our predicament and turned on their exterior lights. Now we could see them, but so could the ground forces. We all hoped the sound of the fighters around the helicopters would discourage ground fire. From Point Hope just off the beach, we ran up the river to Saigon and over to the American Embassy building. On the way, you couldn't miss Vung Tau. It was obviously a city under siege. Flares going off, artillery shells arriving and leaving, mortar impacts, ground fires. And the eerie radio transmissions: voice tones that told of deep desperations more clearly than intelligible words could have.

"Suddenly, we were over Saigon, but I couldn't recognize it. The huge cloud was still overhead, and the lightning added a witches' brew flavor to the ghostly, blacked-out city. I could see Tan Son Nhut airport only when the lightning flashed. There were several fires scattered throughout the town. More artillery and mortar. More desperate voices on the radio. The city was dying. I glanced north toward Bien Hoa just 18 miles away where I had spent a year, and where the VC (Vietcong) now, presumably, slept in my old hootch. I got some sad on me. I mean some jaw-breaking, teary-eyed sad. When 45,000 (sic) good men do the big PCS bit, something permanent is supposed to come of it."

Bombers & Attack Planes Quiz

1. The Boeing B-52 Stratofortress, nicknamed BUFF or Big Ugly Flying "Fellow" (a euphemism for another word starting with F), was designed to carry nuclear weapons. The B-52 was modified internally and externally to carry conventional high explosive bombs. What was the maximum bombload?

A. 10,000 lbs. of bombs
B. 14,000 lbs. of bombs
C. 27,000 lbs of bombs
D. 40,000 lbs of bombs

2. In the air war over Vietnam, Soviet-built Vietnamese Air Force MiG's shot down American aircraft, and vice versa. Navy attack (not fighter) aircraft, on three separate occasions, downed MiG-17's. The victors were of two types. Choose two answers:

A. A-1 Skyraiders (propeller-driven)
B. A-4 Skyhawk (jet)
C. A-6 Intruder (jet)
D. A-7 Corsair II (jet)

This is an Air Force Attack Aircraft identification Test. Identify the two planes pictured here.

3. LTV A-7 Corsair II (or SLUF)
4. Cessna A-37 Dragonfly

A

B

Answers:
1. D
2. A, B
3. A
4. B

FORWARD AIR CONTROLLERS

Forward Air Controllers were generally ex-fighter pilots who directed the fire of attack aircraft or artillery from their flimsy, slow, at best lightly armed, aircraft. They circled over dangerous areas of heavy enemy fire, calling destruction down on the enemy and his weapons, at enormous risk.

O-1 Bird Dog

This small plane, similar to many civilian lightplanes, went into battle armed with smoke rockets and the personal weapons carried by its pilot and observer, but could call upon enormous firepower from firebases and helicopter and fixed-wing aircraft.

Manufacturer: Cessna
Former designation: L-19 (Army); OE-1 (Marines)
Crew: 2
Dimensions: Wingspan: 36 ft.; Length: 25 ft., 9 in.;
Height: 7 ft., 4 in.
Weight: 2,400 lbs. fully loaded
Speed: 115 mph max.
Armament: 4 Smoke rockets
Services using: USAF, USMC, U.S. Army, VNAF

Captain Hilliard A. Wilbanks often flew over the central highlands near Bao Lac and Di Linh. These small cities, located 100 miles northeast of Saigon, were surrounded by a rolling, forested countryside and an occasional plantation. The tribal Montagnards or "mountain people" were the chief inhabitants of the region.

On February 24, 1967, the countryside around Di Linh was not tranquil. The 23rd South Vietnamese Ranger Battalion sought the enemy. They were not alone in the search. A small detachment of American advisers accompanied them, and Americans also patrolled the skies. US Army helicopter gunships hovered nearby while overhead a US Air Force FAC, Hilliard Wilbanks, scanned the terrain that lay before the advancing Rangers.

The Vietcong were ready. The night before they had prepared the perfect ambush site. Local tea plantation workers had been "per-

suaded" to help them dig foxholes and bunkers on the hills west of Di Linh. From these camouflaged positions they would wreak havoc on February 24.

Early in the day, the VC had decimated one platoon of South Vietnamese troops and hit two other companies hard from the hillside trap. American advisers had been killed, and vital communications gear had been destroyed. Radio contact, that could have warned the advancing 23rd Vietnamese Rangers of the deadly ambush, was no longer possible. As dusk approached, the trap was set again.

By February 24th, Hilliard Wilbanks had completed ten months of the one-year tour in South Vietnam. As evening approached, he was aloft in his O-1 on his 488th combat mission, contacting Army Captain R.J. Wooten, the senior American adviser with the 23rd Vietnamese Rangers. Captain Wilbanks was also in radio contact with two helicopter gunships hovering west of Di Linh.

As the Rangers advanced slowly through the plantation, the low tea bushes offered them no protective cover. Above, Captain Wilbanks searched the familiar terrain with efficient, probing eyes trained in combat. Suddenly, he saw the trap. The enemy was hidden in camouflaged foxholes on the hillsides; the Rangers were moving toward the ambush. Captain Wooten's radio crackled with the FAC's warning just as the hillsides erupted with enemy fire. The trap was sprung again.

Later, Captain Wooten said, "My lead elements, working their way up the slope, were unaware of the VC positions just ahead until Captain Wilbanks told us. Realizing their ambush was discovered, the VC opened up on my forces and the two FAC planes above with mortars, machine guns, automatic rifles, and countless shoulder weapons. Two of my companies were pinned down and the forward elements suffered heavy casualties."

Overhead the Bird Dog banked and turned as Hilliard fired a white phosphorous rocket toward the center of the enemy fire. The marking smoke rose from the hillside, pinpointing the ambush site, and the two helicopter gunships wheeled toward the enemy, fired rapidly, and pulled away. A third chopper was hit by .50-caliber fire, which damaged its hydraulic system. Wilbanks advised the remaining pair of gunships to escort the crippled craft to friendly territory. A second FAC radioed that two flights of fighters were on the way.

Then Captain Wilbanks saw movement. The Vietcong had abandoned their foxholes. With bayonets and knives ready, they charged down the slope toward the badly outnumbered Rangers. There was scant hope for help from the air since the gunships had departed and the fighters would not arrive in time.

The FAC was overhead once more. A smoke rocket exploded amidst the enemy force. The Vietcong turned their attention skyward and sent a hail of bullets toward the fleeing Bird Dog. Again Wilbanks banked his plane toward the enemy. He had their full attention now as another smoke rocket slammed into the hillside. The Bird Dog had become the hunter! Yet another low pass followed, and again intense groundfire threatened the aircraft. Wilbanks fired another rocket, his last.

He had one threat left in the automatic rifle that he carried as a survival weapon. Now Captain Wilbanks became both a pilot and a rifleman. Pointing the O-1 toward the enemy, he released the controls and fired his rifle from the side window. As the Bird Dog careened above the tree tops, he grabbed the controls to recover the plane and evade the enemy's fire. Now the Vietcong were off-balance and confused. The FAC reloaded another clip and attacked again. "Each pass he was so close we could hear his plane being hit," said Captain Wooten. The second FAC tried to contact Captain Wilbanks, but there was no reply. On the third rifle-firing pass, the aerial ballet ended.

A Ranger adviser, Captain Gary F. Vote said, "He was no more than 100 feet off the ground and almost over his objective, firing his rifle. Then he began the erratic moves, first up, then down, then banking west right over my position. I thought he was wounded and looking for a friendly spot to land. I jumped up and waved my arms. But as he banked again, I could see that he was unconscious. His aircraft crashed about 100 meters away."

Captain Wilbanks was alive when Captain Vote pulled him from the wreckage. Meanwhile, the two helicopter gunships that doubled as rescue birds returned. They fired their remaining ammunition into the enemy positions and swooped low toward the fallen Bird Dog to pick up the FAC. Four times the Vietcong guns drove them off.

Under the direction of another FAC, two Phantom fighters raked the enemy with 20-millimeter cannon fire. At last a helicopter, braving the withering groundfire, picked up Hilliard Wilbanks. He died in the chopper en route to the treatment center at Bao Lac.

O-2
Super Skymaster

A militarized version of the popular Super Skymaster, the 0-2 was not only larger and faster than its predecessor, but had two engines, allowing flight even if one was lost. Miniguns, 7.62-mm versions of the Gatling-style Vulcan cannon, mounted in underwing pods, gave it offensive power.

Manufacturer: Cessna
Crew: 2
Dimensions: Wingspan: 38 ft.; Length: 29 ft., 9 in.;
Height: 9 ft., 4 in.
Weight: 4,600 lbs.
Speed: 200 mph max.
Armament: Varies, including: 7.62-mm minigun pod, rockets, flares
Services using: USAF

A Forward Air Controller (FAC) who worked morning missions was Captain Philip R. Smotherman, who saw Kham Duc from all the vantage points — more, in fact, than he desired. He was knowledgeable about the emergency because he had been working the radios in the Americal Division tactical operations center (TOC) as the North Vietnamese offensive against the camp was brewing, and he knew of the desperation of the defenders. He took off from Chu Lai in midmorning, May 12, 1968 in his O-2 and arrived over Kham Duc after about a half-hour flight.

Initially, he was the high-altitude FAC, and after that role he controlled aircraft on one side of the runway. He put his first set of fighters onto a known .50-caliber gun position and silenced the guns with some "very quick and accurate work" from a pair of F-100s. He then controlled a pair of Marine A-4Ds with rockets. While directing the fighters his O-2 was struck by enemy fire, and his right wing tip was shot off. Smotherman lost control of the aircraft ailerons, and the elevator soon bound up. He had only rudder and engines for control.

At first he thought he might be forced to bail out or crash land outside the camp perimeter, but then believed he could land on the airstrip if his luck held out. After having started for the field and begun his descent, he was almost run over by a departing C-123. Dodging the C-123 almost cost him his chance for crash landing on the airstrip.

Smotherman made a controlled crash and subsequently was able to move the O-2 off the runway so that it would not block further

0-2

evacuations. He cut off the switches and jumped out of the airplane, now an enemy artillery target. A moment later he was picked up by a Special Forces sergeant, who rushed him into the A Team command bunker as mortars struck around his aircraft.

Smotherman was then able to work in several instances as a ground FAC, directing the fighters on strikes as close as 30 meters from his bunker. On one such strike, necessary because of the proximity of the enemy, Smotherman got dust in his hair from the concussion and felt the heat of the napalm. During the afternoon he was slightly wounded by enemy mortar fragments. He left Kham Duc on the last passenger-carrying C-130, along with the remainder of the Special Forces leaders and some troops.

OV-10 Bronco

The Bronco was an all-purpose FAC aircraft, with speed, maneuverability, and provision for more armament than earlier aircraft. It could be tricky to fly, however, and downright dangerous to ditch.

Manufacturer: North American Rockwell
Crew: 2
Dimensions: Wingspan: 40 ft.; Length: 41 ft., 7 in.;
Height: 15 ft., 2 in.
Weight: 10,000 lbs. loaded
Speed: 281 mph. max.
Armament: 4 7.62-mm machine guns, 3,600 lb. bombs, rockets
Services using: USAF, USMC

On June 29, 1972, Captain Steve Bennett and his backseat observer, Captain Mike Brown, prepared for a combat mission. Mike was a Marine Corps company commander stationed in Hawaii. He had volunteered for temporary duty in Vietnam to assist Air Force FACs in directing naval gunfire. At about 3 p.m., the Air Force-Marine team took off from Danang Air Base and headed northwest along the coast.

Bronco

Thirty minutes later they arrived at Quang Tri and began to circle beneath a deck of low clouds.

For the next two hours, the OV-10 crew adjusted naval artillery from US ships in the Gulf of Tonkin. Mike's radioed instructions to the heavy cruiser *Newport News* and the destroyer *R.B. Anderson* allowed the ships to pinpoint their fire against positions near Quang Tri.

It was time for Steve to turn the Bronco to the south and head for home when he learned that his relief had been delayed on the ground at Danang. A quick check of the fuel gauges confirmed what Steve already knew. He had enough gas to remain on station for another hour. Steve and Mike went back to work.

A mile to the south, a South Vietnamese platoon of about two dozen men was pinned down at a fork in a creek. Several hundred North Vietnamese Army regulars advanced along the creek bank toward their position. The enemy was supported by a heavy artillery barrage and protected by antiaircraft artillery and heat-seeking surface-to-air (SA 7) missiles. The platoon's situation was desperate when a US Marine ground artillery spotter radioed an emergency call for assistance.

Steve Bennett heard the call and responded immediately, swinging his OV-10 toward the fork in the creek. There were no fighters in the area to help. Naval gunfire would threaten the friendly troops as well as the North Vietnamese. Steve had only his skill, the Bronco's four machine guns, and 2,000 rounds of ammunition to pit against the enemy. He would have to attack at low altitude, where the hostile antiaircraft weapons were most effective. Steve radioed for permission to use his guns and got it.

Each time the FAC dove toward the creek bank, he met heavy return fire. After his fourth strafing pass, the North Vietnamese began to pull back, leaving many of their dead and wounded behind. The Bronco had taken several small arms hits in the fuselage, but Steve decided to press the attack to prevent the enemy from regrouping. As he pulled off after the fifth pass, their luck ran out.

Neither Steve nor Mike had any warning as the SA 7 struck from behind. The OV-10 shuddered as the missile hit the left engine and exploded. Steve struggled to control the aircraft as the cockpit was bombarded with shrapnel and debris. Though the canopy was full of holes, he had not been hit. Mike had minor wounds on his hand, head, and back. Together they surveyed the crippled craft. Much of the left engine was gone, and the left landing gear, which had been retracted in a compartment behind the engine, was now hanging limply in the airstream. Worst of all, they were afire!

Steve knew he must jettison the remaining smoke rockets and the external fuel tank before the fire caused an explosion which could destroy the aircraft. He should jettison the stores immediately, but to do so would endanger the lives of the South Vietnamese Marines who were spread out between his present position and the coast. He began a race against time, heading for open water.

In the meantime, Mike had transmitted a distress message on the emergency radio channel. "May Day! May Day! This is Wolfman four-five with Covey eight-seven. We are in the vicinity of Triple Nickel (Highway 555) and 602, heading out feet wet."

The Bronco was a handful for Steve. He consistently fought the controls to maintain straight and level flight as the remaining engine strained to bank and turn the aircraft. Unable to gain altitude, they passed just 600 feet above the beach and the American ships. Reaching open water at last, Steve jettisoned the fuel tank and rockets as he and Mike prepared to eject.

Looking over his shoulder, Mike discovered that his parachute was gone. "What I saw was a hole about a foot square from the rocket blast, and bits of my parachute shredded up and down the cargo bay," Mike says, "I told Steve I couldn't jump." Suddenly there was hope, as the flames subsided.

Quickly the FAC turned southeast down the coast. The landing strips at Phu Bai and Hue were closest, but the battered Bronco would need the foamed runway and crash equipment at Danang. As they passed the city of Hue, the fire flared again and a pilot in a chase plane confirmed that the OV-10 was dangerously close to exploding.

Realizing that they would never reach Danang and that Mike could not eject without a chute, Steve decided to ditch the Bronco by crash-landing in the water. He knew that an OV-10 pilot had never survived a ditching and that the aircraft was likely to break up in the cockpit area as it struck the water.

Steve eased the aircraft into a slow descent toward the water as the two captains completed their pre-ditching checklist. They touched down about one mile from a sandy beach and Mike remembers, "We dug in harder than hell." The landing gear caught in the sea before the Bronco cartwheeled and flipped over on its back.

In the submerged rear cockpit, Mike labored frantically to free himself. He unstrapped and tried to exit through the top of the canopy. Finding the way blocked, he pulled himself clear through an opening in the side and yanked the toggles to inflate his life preserver. On the surface, Mike found only the aircraft's tail section still afloat.

He swam around the tail but could not find Steve, Mike pulled himself down the tail section and back underwater, fighting to reach the front cockpit. He got only as far as the wing, and when he surfaced for the second time, the OV-10 had gone under. A few minutes later, at about 7 p.m., Mike Brown was picked up by a Navy rescue helicopter.

The next day, June 30th, Steve Bennett's body was recovered from the smashed cockpit of the submerged aircraft. He had had no chance to escape.

FAC Quiz

1. Identify the plane shown here.

A. Cessna O-1 "Bird Dog"
B. Cessna O-2 "Super Skymaster"
C. North American Rockwell OV-10 "Bronco"

Match these examples of pilot jargon with their meanings:

2. _____ Six   A. Fuel tanks nearly empty
3. _____ Bingo   B. Warning for anti-radiation
                                  missile launch
4. _____ Pucker Factor   C. Position right behind you
5. _____ Shotgun   D. Graphic description of
                                  fear

Answers:
1. C
2. C
3. A
4. D
5. B

AIRLIFT AND CARGO GUNSHIPS

Airlift of men and material was an often hazardous mission. Enemy fire was a constant hazard, particularly at firebases or villages attacked by the Vietcong or North Vietnamese, and damaged or destroyed many cargo planes. Modified cargo gunships fought back, with armament up to 40-mm cannon and 105-mm howitzers on AC-130's.

The largest cargo plane which could land at short, unimproved fields, the Hercules supplied many bases with the necessities. At Khe Sanh, they parachuted many cargoes, and dropped others off in innovative ways under fire. AC-130 gunships armed with 105-mm howitzers, among other weapons, were death to many trucks on the Ho Chi Minh Trail.

Manufacturer: Lockheed-Georgia
Crew: 5, 92 passengers
Dimensions: Wingspan: 132 ft., 7 in.; Length: 98 ft.; Height: 38 ft., 6 in.
Weight: 108,000 lbs. fully loaded
Speed: 331 mph cruising
Services using: USAF, USMC, VNAF

C-130 Hercules

On February 10, 1968, a tragedy occurred at Khe Sanh which resulted in a drastic alteration of the unloading of supplies from C-130 transports. A Marine C-130, heavily laden with bladders of fuel for the 26th Marines, was making its approach to the field under intense fire. Just before the giant bird touched down, the cockpit and fuel bags were riddled by enemy bullets. With flames licking at one side, the stricken craft careened off the runway 3,100 feet from the approach end, spun around, and was rocked by several muffled explosions. The C-130 then began to burn furiously. Crash crews rushed to the plane and started spraying it with foam. The pilot, Chief Warrant Officer Henry Wildfang, and his copilot suffered minor burns as they scrambled out the overhead hatch in the cockpit. Fire fighters in specially designed heat suits dashed into the flaming debris and pulled several injured crewmen and passengers to safety — rescue attempts came too late for six others. As a result of this accident and damage sustained by other transports while on the ground, C-130 landings at Khe Sanh were suspended.

With the field closed to C-130s, a U.S. Air Force innovation — the Low Altitude Parachute Extraction System or LAPES — was put into effect. This self-contained system, which had been used extensively during the renovation of the airstrip in the fall of 1967, enabled the aircraft to unload their cargo without landing. When making a LAPES run, the Hercules pilot made his approach from the east during which he opened the tail ramp and deployed a reefed cargo parachute. Prior to touchdown, he added just enough power to hold the aircraft about five feet above the ground. As the plane skimmed over the runway and approached the intended extraction point, the pilot electrically opened the streaming chute which was attached to the roller-mounted cargo pallets. The sudden jolt of the blossoming chute snatched the cargo from the rear hatch and the pallets came to a skidding halt on the runway. The pilot then jammed the throttles to the firewall, eased back on the yoke, and executed a high-angle, westerly pull-out to avoid ground fire while the Marines moved onto the runway with forklifts and quickly gathered in the supplies. Even though the airmen could not control the skidding pallets after release, some pilots perfected their individual technique and were able to place the cargo on a 25-meter square with consistency. On one occasion, however, an extraction chute malfunctioned and the cargo rocketed off the western end of the runway; the eight-ton pallet of lumber smashed into a messhall located near the end of the strip and crushed three Marines to death.

Another technique — the Ground Proximity Extraction System or GPES — was also used but to a lesser degree than the LAPES. Both utilized the low approach but with GPES the cargo was extracted by a hook extended from a boom at the rear of the aircraft. As the C-130 swooped low over the runway, the pilot tried to snag an arresting cable similar to the one used on aircraft carriers; only his hook was attached to the cargo bundles and not the plane. Upon engagement, the pallets were jerked from the rear hatch and came to a dead stop on the runway. With the GPES, the chance of a pallet skidding out of control or overturning was greatly reduced. The only problem that occurred was not with the system itself but with faulty installation. The Marines who initially emplaced the GPES were frequently chased away from their work by incoming mortar rounds and, as a result of the periodic interruptions, the cable was not anchored properly. The first C-130 that snagged the wire ripped the arresting gear out by the roots. After the initial bugs were remedied, the system worked so successfully that, on one pass, a load containing 30 dozen eggs was extracted without a single eggshell being cracked.

C-5A Galaxy

The giant C-5A, largest aircraft in the Free World, arrived late on the scene in Vietnam. It carried large cargoes, such as tanks, helicopters and aircraft, or large numbers of personnel.

Manufacturer: Lockheed-Georgia
Crew: 5
Dimensions: Wingspan: 222 ft., 8 in.; Length: 247 ft.;
Height: 65 ft., 1 in.
Weight: 765,000 lbs. fully loaded
Service using: USAF

On Friday, April 4, 1975, an unusual opportunity to evacuate 40-50 American employees from South Vietnam was identified when word received that a C-5A carrying weapons for the South Vietnamese forces was reported inbound. The entire aircraft would be available for the evacuation of passengers and orphans. In a frenzy of activity and coordination, 37 secretaries and analysts of the Defense Attache Office, all women, were selected to serve as escorts for about 250 orphans to be moved under Operation "Babylift." In midafternoon, the aircraft delivered its cargo of 17 105-mm howitzers, and the entire unloading operation was filmed by Vietnamese and American TV crews. The Vietnamese Air Force stated that the purpose of the filming was to demonstrate to the Vietnamese people that the US was still supporting the Thieu government. At the same time, however, the humanitarian "Babylift" was fully covered as orphans and sponsors were hurriedly loaded aboard the aircraft. The aircraft departed Tan Son Nhut without incident. At 23,000 feet during climbout and 10 miles off the Vietnamese coast near Vung Tau, the C-5 experienced a massive structural failure in the rear cargo door area.

In a considerable feat of airmanship, Captain Dennis Traynor and his crew nursed the aircraft back over Saigon and attempted to make an emergency landing at Tan Son Nhut. The explosive decompression had blown out a huge section of the cargo ramp and door and cut all control cables to the rudder and elevator. Using only ailerons (and engine power for pitch control) Captain Traynor was forced to crash land in rice paddies about five miles short of the Tan Son Nhut runway. The aircraft touched down initially on the east side of the Saigon River, bounced and flew about one-half mile across the river where it touched down again and broke up into four major sections. From the crew compartment, upper passenger compartment, and the remnants of the fuselage section, 175 survivors of the crash were able to climb out. The crew members, after freeing themselves, assisted in pulling other survivors from the aircraft wreckage. Within minutes of the crash, Air America and Vietnamese Air Force helicopters from Tan Son Nhut and Bien Hoa were on the scene rescuing survivors. Later they recovered the bodies of those killed in the crash.

The first four days in April, 1975 ended on a tragic note. The inevitable full-scale evacuation of all Americans from South Vietnam had begun.

C-123 Provider

Developed from an all-metal glider prototype, the C-123 could take off and land from short, unimproved airfields, a useful trait in serving small bases throughout South Vietnam and Laos.

Manufacturer: Fairchild
Crew: 2 pilots, 60 passengers
Dimensions: Wingspan: 110 ft.; Length: 76 ft., 3 in.;
Height: 34 ft., 1 in.
Weight: 60,000 lbs. fully loaded
Speed: 245 mph max.
Services using: USAF, VNAF

Although performing important work as transports in Vietnam, the C-123s are best remembered for their defoliation spraying missions under the Air Force Ranch Hand program from 1961 to 1971.

Ranch Hand C-123s began spraying defoliation herbicides on a four-target complex of rivers at the extreme southern tip of the Ca Mau peninsula in the middle of April, 1964. This group of targets included the Cha La area. The Vietcong had controlled two of the target areas for more than three years, and in an attempt to reduce the effectiveness of ground fire. Ranch Hand crews utilized the recently developed "pop-up" tactic. This tactic involved flying at the extremely low altitude of 20 feet over the flat Delta land between spray targets, climbing to the 150-foot spray release altitude just before reaching the spray-on point, and descending again to 20 feet in order to exit the target area. Before April 30, this tactic was able to keep the average number of hits to about three to five per mission.

On April 30, 1964, Ranch Hand flew a spray mission against a target in the Delta which they had selected from the approved list after Major General Joseph H. Moore, the commander of the 2d Air Division (Air Force headquarters in South Vietnam), asked them to pick a spray target where they could guarantee that they would receive ground fire. A special escort of four VNAF A-1 fighters, each with a single VNAF pilot, and four VNAF T-28 fighters with mixed USAF and VNAF crews was authorized for this mission.

The fighters rendezvoused with two Ranch Hand C-123s about an hour before sunrise over Tan Son Nhut for the flight south. At first light they arrived over their target, a canal. Captain Charles F. Hagerty, the Ranch Hand commander at that time, flew lead, and Captain

Eugene D. Stammer piloted the second aircraft. One plane sprayed one side of the canal; the other took the opposite bank.

Ranch Hand's promised ground fire, much more intense than expected, burst forth near a small village. Just as they reached the village, Captain Hagerty felt what he thought was his airplane exploding. Two .50-caliber machine guns, one on either side of the canal, opened up on his lead aircraft and "walked" it down the canal in a crossfire. The crews also reported possible air-burst mortar fire. On Hagerty's plane, one of the two engines was hit. Hagerty immediately feathered it and dumped the remaining herbicide load while climbing for altitude. Another round of enemy fire came up through the oxygen regulator, penetrated the right armrest, and disintegrated in the copilot's parachute where it started a fire, indicating that it was probably a tracer round. The copilot was burned, and the navigator received minor scratches while beating out the fire in the copilot's parachute.

Captain Stammer also immediately turned off the target, gained altitude, and called for rescue helicopters on ground alert. The accompanying fighters strafed the suspected gun positions and also received .50-caliber fire, although they took no losses. Hagerty nursed his damaged C-123 into an airstrip at Soc Trang, and Stammer landed to pick up him and his crew and take them back to Saigon. They discovered that Hagerty's plane, later known as "Patches," had 40 holes in it while Stammer's plane had 10 or 12 hits, all from .50-caliber guns.

KC-135 Stratotanker

Based on the proven Boeing 707 airliner, the KC-135 was the jet successor to the firm's KC-97 and KB-50 tankers, both also modified from cargo or bomber designs. The boom operator rode face-down and backwards and maneuvered the movable boom to lock up with the fuel intakes of the trailing aircraft.

Manufacturer: Boeing
Crew: 4
Dimensions: Wingspan: 130 ft., 10 in.;
Length: 136 ft., 3 in.;
Height: 38 ft., 4 in.
Weight: 296,000 lbs. loaded
Speed: 585 mph max.
Armament: none
Service using: USAF

The "gas station in the sky" was the accepted nickname for the KC-135 Strato-tanker long before Vietnam, and it was ideal for the task of refueling both bomber and fighter aircraft in Southeast Asia. The military version of Boeing's 707, it is a high-speed, high-altitude bird capable of offloading any or all of its 30,000 gallons-plus fuel capacity.

Airborne refueling in direct support of combat operations was the primary mission of the tanker force and included both pre-strike and post-strike refuelings. It also included fuel for fighters flying MIG cover and ground fire suppression for rescue operations, photo reconnaissance and electronic intelligence aircraft, and, on occasions, Navy aircraft.

The term "save" was used to reflect an air refueling with a receiver which had insufficient fuel to return to his base. In early 1965, the nickname Young Tiger was given to KC-135s refueling tactical fighters and reconnaissance aircraft in Southeast Asia. Young Tiger came to be a nickname revered by the consumer and borne proudly by the tanker crews. The "Save Scrapbook" of the 4252nd Strategic Wing

contains the account of a battle-damaged fighter who was losing more fuel than the tanker was offloading to him. The tanker towed the fighter back to his base with its boom, unlatching him on final approach.

Strategic Air Command KC-135 tankers compiled an admirable record of saves of tactical aircraft and their crews.

On July 5, 1966 one of the most remarkable of these feats occurred, referred to as the "Peanuts Flight." This was a flight of four F-105s which had penetrated deep into North Vietnam and got into a fight with MIG aircraft, consuming a good deal more fuel than expected. In response to an emergency call, a tanker headed for them at maximum speed. When the tanker closed in, the F-105s had between 200 to 500 pounds of fuel remaining in their tanks. Two of the pilots in fact, were just about resigned to abandoning their aircraft, but were talked into trying to hookup. The tanker hooked up first with No. 4 who by then had only 100 pounds of fuel on board. So desperate was he that he made the hookup in a left hand 30 degree bank and took on just enough fuel to keep going. By this time the lead F-105's fuel gauges indicated "empty," so the tanker gave him a token load.

In this manner the tanker rotated with all four fighters, first giving each just enough to keep going until the others got a share and then providing sufficient fuel to all for a safe return to home base. This KC-135 surely saved all four valuable aircraft and very probably the lives of their crews as well. Its crew was from the 301st Air Refueling Squadron, under command of Captain Howard G. Stalnecker.

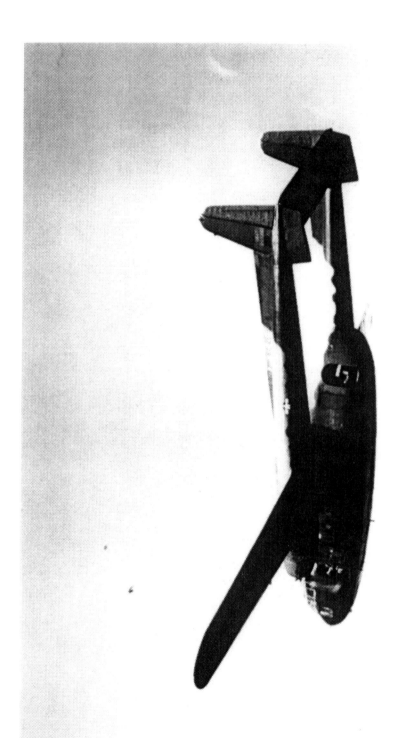

C-119 Flying Boxcar
AC-119 Stinger

Following the pattern of the AC-47, the AC-119 was an altered cargo aircraft, but larger and more powerful than the Spooky. Its high wing allowed a better field of fire for the heavy armament. AC-119 Shadows also destroyed many trucks along the Ho Chi Minh Trail. The C-119K Stinger had two turbojets added to the G model's two piston engines.

Manufacturer: Fairchild
Crew: 8 (C-119G); 10 (C-119K)
Dimensions: Wingspan: 149 ft.; Length: 95 ft., 8 in.;
Height: 32 ft.
Weight: 77,000 lb. fully loaded
Speed: 240 mph max.
Armament: 4 7.62-mm miniguns, 2 20-mm Vulcan cannon
Services using: USAF, VNAF

The night of May 8, 1970, witnessed an extraordinary display of airmanship when a C-119 Stinger from Udorn was heavily damaged by antiaircraft fire:

Captain Alan D. Milacek and his nine-man crew had been reconnoitering a heavily defended road section near Ban Ban, Laos, when they discovered, attacked and destroyed two trucks. Captain James A. Russell and Captain Ronald C. Jones, the sensor operators, located three more trucks. As the aircraft banked into attack orbit, six enemy positions opened up with a barrage of AA fire. The copilot Captain Brent C. O'Brien, cleared the fighter escort for attack and the gunship circled as the F-4s worked to suppress the AA Fire. Amid the heavy enemy fire, Captain Milacek resumed the attack and killed another truck. At 0100, just about 2 hours into the mission, "the whole cargo compartment lit up" as enemy rounds tore into the Stinger's right wing. A "sickening right dive of the aircraft" ensued and Milacek called "Mayday, Mayday, we're goin' in." He shouted orders to Staff Sergeant Adolfo Lopez, Jr., the IO (illuminator operator), to jettison the flare launcher.

Captain Milacek directed the entire crew to get ready for instant bailout. As the gunship dropped about 1,000 feet within a few seconds, Captains Milacek and O'Brien pooled their strength to pull the aircraft out of its dive. By using full-left rudder, full-left aileron, and maximum power on the two right engines, they regained stabilized flight. The full-engine power fueled 2- to 3-foot flames — torchlights for enemy gunners as the crippled Stinger desperately headed for friendly territory. The navigator Captain Roger E. Clancy gave the correct heading but warned they were too low to clear a range of mountains towering between them and safety. What's more, the crew discovered that fuel consumption would likely mean dry tanks before reaching base.

The crew tossed out every possible item to lighten the load and the aircraft slowly climbed to 10,000 feet. Technical Sergeant Albert A. Nash, the flight engineer, reported the fuel-consumption rate had fallen. Captain Milacek elected to land the damaged plane and when he approached the base area he ran a careful check of controls. He found that almost full-left rudder and aileron would allow him to keep control. With uncertain flap damage, Milacek chose a no-flap landing approach at 150 knots (normally 117 knots). Utilizing every bit of pilot skill, he landed the plane. Upon leaving the Stinger, the crew saw about one-third of the right wing (a 14-foot section and aileron) had been torn off.

AC-47 Spooky

The World War II workhorse C-47 found a new role in Vietnam when the Air Force modified some into AC-47's. The A was for "attack", though some wits said it stood for "ancient". These craft orbited over firebases and villages attacked by Vietcong, dropping illumination flares and blazing away with side-mounted miniguns.

Manufacturer: Douglas
Unofficial name: Spooky, Puff the Magic Dragon
Crew: 7
Dimensions: Wingspan: 90 ft.; Length: 67 ft., 9 in.;
Height: 18 ft., 3 in.
Weight: 31,000 lb. (C-47, fully loaded)
Speed: 270 mph max.
Armament: 3 7.62-mm miniguns
Services using: USAF, VNAF (C-47 used by USAF, USN, USMC, VNAF)

On the evening of February 24, 1969, an AC-47 with the call sign "Spooky 71" lifted off the runway at Bien Hoa Air Base. As the Gooney Bird climbed into the clear night sky, her eight-man crew prepared for a long combat air patrol mission in the Saigon area. In the cargo compartment, the crew's loadmaster, Airman First Class John L. Levitow, was airborne on his 180th combat mission.

One of John's responsibilities on the gunship was handling the Mark 24 flares. He would set the ejection and ignition controls and pass the flare to the gunner, Airman Ellis C. Owen, who attached it to a lanyard. On the pilot's command, Owen would simultaneously pull the safety pin and toss the flare through the open cargo door.

The Mark 24 looked innocent enough. It was a three-foot-long metal tube weighing 27 pounds. Ten seconds after release an explosive charge deployed a parachute. In another ten seconds the magnesium flare would ignite, quickly reaching a temperature of 4,000 degrees Fahrenheit and illuminating the countryside with two million candlepower. Drifting slowly beneath its chute, each flare would burn for over a minute.

The Vietcong guerrillas, peasants by day and terrorists by night, were denied the protection of darkness when Spooky was about.

Spooky 71 and her crew had been airborne for 4½ hours when the pilot, Major Ken Carpenter, received word of enemy action around Bien Hoa. As Carpenter wheeled the Gooney Bird back toward its home field, he and his copilot saw muzzle flashes from the perimeter of the Long Binh Army Base below. The Vietcong were busy here, also.

The gunship circled in an orbit centered around the muzzle flashes. In two lightning-quick attacks with mini-guns chattering, she slammed 3,000 rounds of ammunition into the enemy positions. Spooky 71 received an urgent request to remain in the vicinity to provide illumination for friendly ground forces.

Major Carpenter received a second call requesting illumination in an area two miles south of Long Binh. As the aircraft swung to the south, the pilots saw flashes from a heavy mortar barrage ahead. The crew in the cargo compartment followed the sounds of the action. Later, John Levitow recalled, "Every once in a while, you'd hear a muffled noise when a mortar hit. You could hear the engines on the aircraft, the noise of the guns firing and the pilot giving instructions."

Suddenly, Spooky 71 was jarred by a tremendous explosion and bathed in a blinding flash of light. The crew would learn later that

a North Vietnamese Army 82-millimeter mortar shell had landed on top of the right wing and exploded inside the wing frame. The blast raked the fuselage with flying shrapnel.

In the cockpit the pilots struggled to bring the lurching Gooney Bird under control. They had been momentarily blinded, and the navigator, Major William Platt recalls, "Even in the navigation compartment, the flash lit up the inside of the aircraft like daylight. The aircraft veered sharply to the right and down." Though the situation was desperate in the cockpit, it was even worse in the cargo compartment.

Sergeant Edward Fuzie, who was wounded in the back and neck, remembers, "I saw Sergeant Baer, Airman Owen, and Airman Levitow go down right away. Baer was covered with blood."

John Levitow thought one of the mini-guns had exploded. In his words, "But when I was actually hit, the shrapnel felt like a two-by-four, or a large piece of wood which had been struck against my side. It stung me. I really didn't know what it was."

Airman Owen was the first to realize that the Spooky crew was still in mortal danger. "I had the lanyard on one flare hooked up, and my finger was through the safety pin ring. When we were hit, all three

of us were thrown to the floor. The flare, my finger still through the safety pin ring, was knocked out of my hand. The safety pin was pulled and the flare rolled on the aircraft floor, fully armed!"

Major Carpenter learned via the intercom that everyone in the back was wounded and a live flare was loose in the plane. In the meantime, John Levitow came to the aid of a fellow crewmember, who was perilously close to the open cargo door. As he dragged his buddy back toward the center of the cabin, John saw the flare.

The canister rolled crazily amidst the ammunition cans which contained over 19,000 rounds of live ammunition. In less than 20 seconds the AC-47 would become a flaming torch, plunging its crews to destruction in the night sky. John had no way of knowing how many seconds remained. The beating the flare had already taken could have damaged the timer, causing ignition before the 20 seconds had elapsed. He was weak from loss of blood and numb from the 40 wounds on his right side. But John knew he was the closest to the flare.

Time and again the smoking tube eluded his grasp as the aircraft pitched and rolled. In desperation, he threw himself on the flare and

A versatile, venerable C-47 in camouflage colors takes off from base in South Vietnam.

painfully dragged it toward the cargo door, leaving a trail of blood behind. The seconds ticked by. With a final superhuman effort John heaved the flare through the door. It barely cleared the aircraft before igniting in an incandescent blaze.

Major Carpenter recalls, "I had the aircraft in a 30-degree bank and how Levitow ever managed to get to the flare and throw it out, I'll never know." As he finally brought the ship back to straight and level flight, Major Carpenter headed toward Bien Hoa. He radioed for an ambulance and a medical evacuation helicopter to meet the gunship.

Major Carpenter spoke later about John Levitow and the Gooney Bird. "After the mission I was able to reconstruct what happened by the blood trail left by John. He collapsed after throwing the flare overboard and was evacuated to the base hospital immediately upon landing. It was not possible to bail out as we had two seriously injured men aboard, one of them John Levitow. How the plane ever flew back to the base, I'll never know. How a plane with over 3,500 holes in the wings and fuselage stayed airborne defies description. One hole measured 3 feet, ¼ inches."

Airlift & Cargo Gunships Quiz

1. Identify the plane shown here.

A. Air Force EC-121 Constellation
B. C-47

2. In the Vietnam air war, aerial refueling, in which Air Force or Navy tanker aircraft pumped fuel into other airplanes in flight:

A. Was never used due to the short distances the attack
    airplanes had to fly
B. Allowed attack planes to take off with higher bomb loads. The
    fuel tanks were then topped off by tanker aircraft
C. Was sometimes used to keep damaged aircraft returning from
    raids from running out of fuel which leaked out of
    perforated fuel tanks
D. B and C above
E. None of the above

Glossary

Ace — Combat pilot credited with five or more victories over enemy aircraft.

Afterburner — An auxiliary combustion chamber in the aft section of a jet engine where the unused oxygen of exhaust gases is used to burn a second fuel spray resulting in increased thrust.

Aileron — A control surface on the wing, used to control the rolling movements of the airplane.

Air Defense Command or Aerospace Defense Command — A major air command of the USAF, responsible for providing air defense of the US.

Antiaircraft artillery (AAA) — Projectile weapons with their related equipment, as searchlights, radar, etc., employed on the ground or on ships to strike at airborne aircraft.

Arc Light — Operational name for B-52 strikes in South Vietnam.

Autorotation — The free rotation of rotor blades without engine power; the unpowered descent of a helicopter.

Aviation cadet — A person in training to become a commissioned AF officer with an aeronautical rating.

Bailout — An escape from an aircraft by parachuting.

Barrel roll — Most recently, Barrel Roll refers to strikes against personnel and equipment from North Vietnam.

Bear — Nickname for the backseat electronic warfare officer in certain USAF fighter airplanes.

Bingo — Minimum fuel necessary to reach an airfield.

Bingo field — The only airfield reachable with minimum fuel.

Ceiling — The maximum height at which an airplane or aircrew can fly; the height of the lower surface of a cloud layer.

Chopper — Nickname for helicopter, a craft which does not fly, but "beats the air into submission."

Close air support — Air support provided to friendly surface forces, consisting of air attacks with guns, bombs, guided airborne missiles or rockets on hostile surface forces, their installations or vehicles so close to surface operations as to require detailed coordination between air and friendly forces.

Cluster bombs — Many small bombs carried in a single container or dispenser.

Coast-in — Crossing the enemy coastline.

Counterinsurgency — Operations against a nonregular or guerrilla force.

Crown — Airborne control center coordinating search and rescue efforts; typically a C-54 Skymaster, later C-130 Hercules.

Defense suppression — Military operations to neutralize or destroy the enemy's defensive systems.

Delta wings — Triangular aircraft wings, resembling the Greek letter Delta.

Ditch — To force-land an aircraft on water with the intention of abandonment.

Dust-off — Army designation for Medevac medical evacuation rescue helicopter flights.

Ejection seat — A seat designed to catapult a flyer from an airplane.

Elevator — Horizontal control surface on tail of an aircraft which moves the airplane up or down in flight.

Endurance (aircraft) — The aircraft's ability to remain airborne without in-flight refueling.

Escort — Airplane(s) flying to provide protection for other aircraft.

Face curtain — A movable shield which a pilot pulls down in front of his face when ejecting to protect himself from the onrushing wind.

Feet dry — Code signal to indicate aircraft crossing enemy coastline inbound.

Feet wet — Pilot radio terminology which means he is heading toward or flying over open water.

USAF F-4
Phantom

Final approach — The last leg of a landing pattern, during which the aircraft is lined up with the runway and is held to a fairly constant speed and rate of descent.

Firewall — A structure which separates the pilot's cockpit from the aircraft engine.

Flak — Explosive projectiles fired from antiaircraft guns.

Flaps — Control surfaces often found on the trailing edge of a wing which increase the lift or drag of an airplane.

Flareship — Aircraft which dispenses illuminating flares for night operations.

Flight leader — A pilot in command of a flight of aircraft.

Forward air controller (FAC) — A pilot responsible for directing aircraft to targets by radio in a close-air-support operation.

Gooney Bird — Unofficial name for the C-47, dated from World War II.

Ground controlled approach (GCA) — An instrument approach for landing in reponse to radio directions from a controller observing the aircraft on a radar set.

Groundfire — Fire, such as antiaircraft fire, that emanates from the ground.

Gunships — Helicopters or cargo aircraft modified with guns for a ground attack role.

Haiphong — Major coastal port city of North Vietnam.

Hanoi — Capital city of North Vietnam.

Hanoi Hilton — Ironic name for the major prisoner-of-war compound in North Vietnam.

Ho Chi Minh Trail — Supply route from North Vietnam through Laos to South Vietnam. Named after famous North Vietnamese leader.

Insurgency — Nonregular movement against the established government.

Jettison — To throw out or drop, especially in an emergency situation, cargo, bombs, fuel, or armament to lighten or streamline the aircraft.

Jink — To jerk an aircraft about in evasive action.

Koch Fittings — Release mechanism on parachute harness which separates pilot from parachute, especially when landing on water.

Lanyard — A cord which one pulls.

Linebacker I — Nickname for overall interdiction bombing effort in North Vietnam during the spring, summer, and autumn of 1972.

Linebacker II — Nickname for overall bombing effort in North Vietnam in December 1972.

LPA-1 — Personal life raft.

Magazine — A structure or compartment for storing ammunition or explosives.

MIG — A popular designation for certain Russian fighter aircraft designed and developed by Mikoyan and Gurevich.

mm — Millimeter, as in 100-mm AAA.

On guard - guard frequency — Radio frequency used in search and rescue operations.

Ordnance — Military weapons, ammunition, explosives, combat vehicles and battle materiel.

Pallet — A platform or shallow open box for holding supplies or materials for convenient storage or handling.

Paramedic — A medical technician qualified to participate in parachute activities, especially those involving rescue.

PCS bit — To make the ultimate sacrifice.

Pickle — To drop bombs or other ordnance.

Pierced steel planking (PSP) — Metal strips pierced with numerous holes, used as a temporary surface for an airstrip.

Rattlesnake — Warning tone which indicates to pilot that he is detected by enemy radar.

Reconnaissance — Observation of an area to secure information about the terrain, or the weather, or the enemy and his installations.

Red River — Large North Vietnamese river which flows southeast through Hanoi to the Gulf of Tonkin.

Risers — Long straps which connect parachute harness with the canopy.

Rocket pod — A container carrying rocket ammunition usually mounted on a wingtip or under a wing.

Rudder — Vertical control surface on tail of an airplane which moves the airplane to right or left in flight.

SAM — Surface-to-air missile.

Sandy — Designation for A-1 Skyraider when escorting search and rescue missions.

Scramble — To launch aircraft as rapidly as possible. Airplanes and pilots on alert status are ready for the scramble order.

Seat pan — Part of pilot's seat which detaches during ejection; contains survival equipment.

Shrike — Air-to-ground missile that locks on and guides toward a radar signal.

Sidetones — Tones which indicate survival radio is functioning.

Slick — Nickname for an unarmed (except for light defensive armament) helicopter.

Sortie — A single mission flown in an aircraft.

Spad — Nickname and sometimes call sign for A-1E airplanes.

Spooky — Nickname and call sign of AC-47 gunship.

Strafe — To fire an aircraft gun, usually at a ground target.

Strategic Air Command — A major air command of the USAF charged with carrying out strategic air operations.

TAC - Tactical Air Command Controller — Marine Corps designation for airborne Forward Air Controller.

Tanker Aircraft — An aircraft used to refuel others in flight.

Telephone pole — Soviet-built SA-2 surface-to-air missile, which resembles a flying telephone pole after launch.

Tet — Vietnamese Lunar New Year holiday.

Trim — To adjust or balance an aircraft so that it maintains coordinated, balanced flight.

Turns (aircraft) — 180-degree turn — maneuvering an aircraft to reverse course and head in the opposite direction.

Udorn — A U.S. Air Force base in Thailand.

Vietcong (VC) — Communist guerrillas who fought against the government of South Vietnam.

VMA — Marine Attack Squadron.

VMO — Marine Observation Squadron.

White phosphorous (Willie Pete) — A nonmetallic element that burns readily giving off thick, white smoke. Often used in target marking rockets or smoke grenades.

Wild weasel — Fighter aircraft designed to seek out and destroy enemy defenses.

Wingman — A pilot who flies his aircraft in formation with the flight leader's aircraft.

Yoke — The control stick in an aircraft.

Further Reading

The number of books published about the Vietnam air war has increased enormously since the end of the war in the seventies. As an example, Southfarm Press, publisher of this book (www.war-books.com), recently published a second edition of its popular *Vietnam War Facts Quiz* (ISBN: 978-0913337585) because of increased interest in the war. The book has many questions and illustrations concerning the air war.

US Army, Navy, Air Force and Marine Corps official histories and special studies about the war have been published. Commercial publishers continue to issue histories and memoirs about our involvement in Vietnam. Material about the air war continues to be popular.

Personal accounts of Vietnam Service in the air abound. One of the best of the air war is Colonel Jack Broughton's classic *Thud Ridge: F-105 Thunderchief missions over Vietnam*, originally published in 1969 (ISBN: 978-0859791168; 2006 ed.). Colonel Broughton carried a tape recorder in his cockpit on missions over North Vietnam, and the dialogue in his book is dramatic and real.

The flying stories are riveting in Marshall Harrison's 1989 book, *A Lonely Kind of War: Forward Air Controller Vietnam* (ISBN: 978-0891416388; 1997 ed.). He describes what he faced as one of the "Bringers of Death," a special cadre of air force pilots responsible for directing jet fighter-bomber strikes against the enemy.

Masters of the Art: A Fighting Marine's Memoir of Vietnam (ISBN: 978-0891418795; 2005 ed.) is written by Ronald E. Winter, a highly decorated helicopter door gunner who flew over 300 missions in Vietnam. It's a thrilling account of US Marines aggressively counter-punching off the Tet offensive and the siege of Khe Sanh.

Naked in Da Nang (ISBN: 978-0760320761; 2004), by Mike Jackson and Tara Dixon-Engel is stories of Jackson's days in Vietnam as a forward air controller directing air strikes, observing troop movements and choreographing search-and-rescue missions. The stories are told with pride and a dash of irreverence.

Kregg P. J. Jorgenson has written *Acceptable Loss: Point Man Vietnam* (ISBN: 0-8041-0792-0), published in 1991. As part of a Ranger/LRRP team patrolling the jungles of Vietnam, Jorgenson had seen more combat in four months than most soldiers see in a decade. His wounds and his Silver Star guaranteed him safety at the LRRP base camp. Not interested in that, he joined the Air Cavalry and as part of the Air Cav's fast reaction team, answered alarms that would send him scrambling into choppers for nerve-racking flights to reach surrounded comrades.

Squadron/Signal Publishers have many "In Action Books" richly illustrated with photos and drawings of aircraft, ships, armored vehicles and weapons used in Vietnam. In 1982-84 they published Lou Drendel's 3-volume set in one book, *Air War Over Southeast Asia: A Pictorial Record, 1962-1975 — Three Volumes in One*.

The "Men-At-Arms" and "Elite" series published by British publisher Osprey portray the equipment and uniforms used during the Vietnam War.

An anthology of impressions of Vietnam service by many authors appears in *Touring Nam: The Vietnam War Reader*. Originally published in 1985, the book is edited by Martin Greenberg and Augustus Norton. A reprint paperback edition (ISBN: 978-0553279177) was published in 1989.

Chopper Pilot Frank Anton took off to fly another routine mission over Vietnam on January 5, 1968. Shot down and taken captive, he was marched into hell for a five-year journey. He tells his story (with Tommy Denton) in **Why Didn't You Get Me Out? A POW's Nightmare in Vietnam** (ISBN: 978-0312974886; 2000 ed.).

In Ronald J. Glasser M.D.'s honored book, *365 Days* (1971), the doctor tells how as a pediatrician, he was sent to Japan to serve the dependent children in the military population there. He soon realized that the troopers they were pulling off those med evac choppers in Vietnam were only children themselves. Of particular interest to readers of this book, Vietnam Air War, is chapter 13 in *365 Days*, "Choppers" (ISBN: 978-0807615270; 2003 Reissue ed.).

Palace Cobra: A Fighter Pilot in the Vietnam Air War (ISBN: 978-0312353568; 2006) by Ed Rasimus is a gripping combat memoir by a veteran fighter pilot flying the F-4 Phantom. Includes information about the strategic and tactical conduct of the later stages of the Vietnam air war.

Sources of the stories in this book

The stories you've just read in *Vietnam Air War: 25 Rarely Told Stories* have all been taken from US Department of Defense government publications. Look for them at your local public library or ask for the location of the nearest Government Printing Office Depository Library.

The Web Site for the Government Printing Office Depository Library is:

http://www.access.gpo.gov/su_docs/fdlp/libpro.html

There is a link to the catalog of publications currently for sale.

CHOPPERS

UH-1 Gunship
Telfer, Major Gary L., Lt. Col. Lane Rogers, and V. Keith Fleming, Jr. *U.S. Marines in Vietnam: Fighting the North Vietnamese, 1967.* (Washington: History and Museums Division, Headquarters, U.S. Marine Corps, 1984). S/N 008-055-00165-0

UH-1 Medevac
Dorlan, Peter, and James Nanney. *Dust-Off: Army Aeromedical Evacuation in Vietnam.* (Washington: U.S. Army Center for Military History, 1982). S/N 008-020-00903-2

AH-1 Cobra Gunship
CH-47 Chinook
Tolson, Lt. Gen. John J. *Airmobility: 1961-1971.* (Vietnam Studies. 1973). S/N 008-020-00479-1

HH-43 Huskie
HH-53 Super Jolly Green
Tjlford, Earl H., Jr. *Search and Rescue in Southeast Asia, 1961-1975.* (Washington: Office of Air Force Historian, 1980). S/N 008-070-00453-4

HH-3 Jolly Green Giant

Schneider, Maj. Donald K. *Air Force Heroes in Vietnam*. (USAF Southeast Asia Monograph Series, v. VII) (Maxwell AFB, AL: Air University Airpower Research Institute, 1979). S/N008-070-00448-8

CH-46 Sea Knight

Shore, Capt. Moyers S. *Battle for Khe Sanh*. (Washington: headquarters, U.S. Marine Corps, 1969). S/N 008-055-00114-5

FIGHTERS AND FIGHTER BOMBERS

F-4 Phantom II

Christmann, JO2 Timothy J. "Training Paid Off for Aces in Vietnam." *Naval Aviation News*, March-April 1985, pp. 20-21.

F-8 Crusader

"The Natives Were Friendly This Time..." *Approach*, April 1970, pp. 26-28

F-100 Super Sabre
F-105 Thunderchief

Air Force Heroes in Vietnam. (See source for HH-3).

BOMBERS AND ATTACK PLANES

B-52 Stratofortress

Eastman, James N., Walter Hanak, and Lawrence J. Paszek, eds. *Aces and Aerial Victories - The United States Air Force in Southeast Asia, 1965-1973*. (Washington: Office of Air Force History, 1976). S/N 008-070-00365-1. Also: Battle for Khe Sanh (see source for CH-46).

A-1 Skyraider

Search and Rescue in Southeast Asia (see source for HH-43 and HH-53).

A-4 Skyhawk

Case, JOC Bill, and JO3 John Redmond. "Pilots Praise the Sturdy Skyhawk." *Naval Aviation News*, March, 1968, pp. 11-13.

A-6 Intruder

Owen, Lt. Robert S. "Night Strike From the Enterprise." *Naval Aviation News*, June 1967, pp. 9-10.

A-7 Corsair II
LaValle, Lt. Col. A.J.C. *Last Flight From Saigon.* (USAF Southeast Asia Monograph Series, v. IV). (Maxwell AFB, AL: Air University Airpower Research Institute, reprinted 1985).

FORWARD AIR CONTROLLERS

O-1 Bird Dog
OV-10 Bronco
Air Force Heroes in Vietnam. (see source for HH-3).

O-2 Super Skymaster
Gropman, Lt. Col Alan L. *Airpower and the Airlift Evacuation of Kham Duc.* (USAF Southeast Asia Monograph Series, v. V). (Maxwell AFB, AL: Air University Airpower Research Institute, 1979, reprinted 1985). S/N 008-070-00434-8.

AIRLIFT AND CARGO GUNSHIPS

C-130 Hercules
Battle for Khe Sanh (see source for CH-46).

C-5A Galaxy
Last Flight From Saigon (see source for A-7).

C-123 Provider
Buckingham, William A. *Operation Ranch Hand: The United States Air Force and Herbicides in Southeast Asia, 1961-1971.* (Washington: Office of Air Force History, 1982). S/N 008-070-00466-6.

KC-135 Stratotanker
Hopkins, Charles K. *SAC Tanker Operations in the Southeast Asia War.* (Offutt AFB, NE: Headquarters, Strategic Air Command, 1987);
and
LaValle, Maj. A.J.C. *The Tale of Two Bridges and the Battle for the Skies Over North Vietnam.* (Maxwell AFB, AL: Air University Airpower Research Institute, 1976, reprinted 1985). S/N 008-070-00372-4.

AC-119 Stinger
Ballard, Jack S. *Development and Employment of Fixed-Wing Gunships, 1962-1972.* (Washington: Office of Air Force History, 1982). S/N 008-070 00452-6.

AC-47 Spooky
Air Force Heroes in Vietnam. (see source for HH-3).

Printed in the United States
82929LV00002B/1-50/A